MY TRUTH

Indira Gandhi

Presented by Emmanuel Pouchpadass
Based on Interviews and Other Source Material

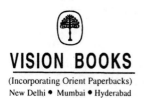

VISION BOOKS

(Incorporating Orient Paperbacks)
New Delhi • Mumbai • Hyderabad

www.vision**books**india.com

ISBN 81-7094-468-6

© Editions Stock, 1980

Published in English by
Vision Books Pvt. Ltd.
(Incorporating Orient Paperbacks and CARING Imprints)
24 Feroze Gandhi Road, Lajpat Nagar III
New Delhi-110024 (India)
in collaboration with
Editions Stock, 14 rue de' Ancienne-
Comedie, 75006 Paris, France
Phone: (+91-11) 2983 6470
Fax: (+91-11) 2983 6490
E-mail: visionbk@vsnl.com

Printed at
Rashtra Rachna Printers
C-88, Ganesh Nagar, Pandav Nagar Complex
Delhi-110092 (India).

All photographs courtesy
Jawaharlal Nehru Memorial
Fund, New Delhi

Contents

...Never do anything in secret or anything that you would wish to hide. For the desire that you want to hide anything means that you are afraid, and fear is a bad thing and unworthy of you. Be brave, and the rest follows. . . .

JAWAHARLAL NEHRU
(In a letter to his daughter written in prison in October 1930 and published in *Glimpses of World History*)

Foreword

THE LONG SERIES OF INTERVIEWS WHICH PRODUCED THIS book began on the tenth anniversary of Mrs. Gandhi's installation as Prime Minister of India. Ten years in the life of a country is not much, but ten years in the life of a Head of State represent a great deal. In addition, looking backwards to draw up a balance sheet is justified.

The object of this book, therefore, is not to answer questions of current interest which certainly would be interesting but which would quickly render the work out of date. Its purpose is to show who Mrs. Gandhi is and how her personality was shaped and the incredible adventure by which she came to govern one-sixth of the world's population. This could only be done by allowing the interested party to express herself fully.

Now it seemed neither possible nor reasonable to ask an active head of government to undertake such a performance. And yet this is what I attempted and what Mrs. Gandhi accepted to do. Unquestionably, this is astonishing when one considers the difficulty of being completely available experienced by those who occupy such high posts. This is due to the exceptional character of the person involved and the view of life which is uniquely her own.

This view could only be revealed by Mrs. Gandhi herself. This is why she has been allowed to express herself for the entire length of the book. The questions serve simply to punctuate and stimulate reflection, to establish links between the times and the events and, finally, to ensure the smooth flow of the account.

Beyond the public personage who has achieved the summit of power described in the press and on television, these interviews have sought to reveal a life and a choice. For, what is obtained through successive touches by means of what Mrs. Gandhi says about her origins, her background, her formation, her childhood dreams, being a young girl and young woman, her aims, her activities, her victories and defeats and, finally, her reactions to events, constitutes both totality and quintessence.

EMMANUEL POUCHPADASS

CHAPTER 1

The Earliest Days

When you were born on 19 November 1917 in Allahabad, located at the junction of the Ganges, the Yamuna and the mythical Saraswati rivers, all the signs were propitious. Your birth took place under the double sign of tenderness and energy. You were named Indira Priyadarshini "she who one loves to look upon". In a letter sent to your father on that occasion, Sarojini Naidu wrote: "This child will be the new soul of India".

At that time, Allahabad was an important cultural and administrative centre and your birthplace, Anand Bhavan, was the residence of one of the most distinguished citizens, Motilal Nehru, your grandfather. Curiously, Allahabad provided an independent India with her first three heads of government. Had India been freed earlier, Motilal Nehru would have also been a Prime Minister.

I WAS BORN ON 19 NOVEMBER 1917, IN OUR BEAUTIFUL HOUSE of Anand Bhavan (the home of happiness) at Allahabad, until recently one of the prominent cultural and administrative centres of India. My family, the Nehrus, were of Kashmiri origin.

I was very fortunate in that I was surrounded by extraordinary people. My grandfather was there, and his personality couldn't be ignored. And the same is true of my father, although he wasn't strong in the same way. But his views were very definite. And then, of course, in the background stood Mahatma Gandhi and other leaders.

As for any other child I suppose, my mother played a very special role. Among all these people, she too had a very strong character. But in a quiet way. And somehow she made a very deep impression. One tends to resist the influence of obviously strong people, and not be so concerned about that of people around them. Yet, if she believed in something, nothing could move her from it.[1]

Many people know the part played by my grandfather and my father. But in my opinion a more important part was played by my mother. When my father wanted to join Gandhiji and to change the whole way of life, to change our luxurious living, to give up his practice, the whole family was against it. It was only my mother's courageous and persistent support and encouragement which enabled him to take this big step which made such a difference not only to our family but to the history of modern India, and I know that this situation must have taken place in many homes in India.

I was surrounded by love and energy. But in spite of the name I was given, Indira Priyadarshini, I would not say — as some have — that I was spoiled. On the contrary, while my grandfather gave in to me on a number of things, he believed in strictness of upbringing. My father and mother, of course, were even stricter in the day to day matters. Except for the very early days, I would say that I had a spartan type of life. And once the family entered the political scene, it became a life of tension and concern for my parents.

I don't really remember our life of luxury in Anand Bhavan. I do recall though that the days there were more leisurely than later. I remember my grandfather's birthday party and things like that.

What I have a very vivid memory of is when we first burnt our foreign clothes. I can still feel the excitement of the day and see the large terrace covered with piles of clothes — what rich materials, what lovely colours! What fun for a toddler to jump on, play hide and seek in the heaps of velvets and satins, silks and chiffons! That was also the day when I discovered my power over my parents. Everybody was going to the bonfire but I was considered too small and was being put to bed. I appealed to my grandfather, who, then as always later, took

---

1. Kamala Nehru had a strong influence on her husband as this letter written by him in 1918 indicates: "I suppose my father and Gandhiji have been the chief personal influences in my life. But outside influences do not carry me away. There is a tendency to resist being influenced. Still influences do work slowly and subconsciously. My wife influenced me considerably in many ways, though unobtrusively."

my side. However, I fell asleep almost as soon as we arrived, seeing only the burning wood thrown on the mountain of clothes and the fire putting forth its first flickering, testing tongue of flame.

A little later I had my first encounter with conscience and duty. Being an only child, I liked to play by myself but I had to have my mother within my range of vision and hearing. One evening she had a visitor, a relative returning from Paris who had brought an exquisite embroidered dress for me. Mummy smilingly returned it saying that we now wore only handspun and handwoven material, *khadi*. The visitor could not understand this, and glancing at my mother's clothes — the only *khadi* available then was thick and rough as sacking — she could not help noticing that wherever her skin had rubbed against the sari it had become sore and red. She burst out, "I think you have all gone mad but you are an adult, and if you want to be ill, I suppose it is your business, but you certainly have no right to make the child suffer and I have brought this gift for her." "Come here, Indu," called my mother. "Aunty has brought you a foreign frock. It is very pretty and you can wear it if you like. But, first, think of the big fire where we burnt our foreign things. Would you like to wear this dainty thing when the rest of us are wearing *khadi*?" The temptation was very strong — my eyes shone with desire — I stretched out a small hand to touch the dress but even before my hand reached it I found myself saying "Take it away — I shan't wear it." "But why not, don't you like nice things?" the visitor teased. "I do... I do... but...," and I repeated all the arguments I had overheard from the elders' talk, when she said: "All right, Miss Saint, how is it that you have a foreign doll?" It was an idle remark, thoughtlessly made. Adults so often look upon children as playthings — not understanding what is hidden by the lack of power of expression. I was passionately fond of the doll. I could not think of it — or indeed of anything — as lifeless. Everything was given a name and immediately developed its own personality — the doll was my friend, my child.

For days on end — or was it weeks? it doesn't matter, it seemed an eternity — I was overwhelmed by the burden of decision — the struggle went on between love for my doll, pride of owning such a lovely thing, and what I thought to be my duty towards my country. Never fond of food, I found it even more irksome then, and sleep came only out of exhaustion. My mother thought I was sick for something and so I was. At last I made my decision and, quivering with tension, I took the doll up on the roof-terrace and set fire to it. Then tears came as if they would never stop and for some days I was ill with a temperature. To this day I hate striking a match.

*   *   *

Our house was beginning its new career as a centre for political activities. There were constant meetings, large and small. My favourite game was to collect as many servants as I could, stand on a table and deliver a speech — repeating disjointed phrases that I had picked up from grown-up talk.

In spite of all these people coming, when I look at it in retrospect, Anand Bhavan was a house of serenity and of a very cosmopolitan nature. It was cosmopolitan, not only in the sense of people of different nationalities and different thoughts but even in terms of the mixture to be found there — British and Indian intellectuals rubbing shoulders with the steady stream of peasants who also came to the house.

Allahabad was the most important town of the most important State of India which was called the United Provinces at that time. Allahabad was an intellectual centre, a cultural centre and a political centre. There lived some of the brightest stars of the judiciary and the legal profession. The Allahabad University had a very high standing in the country so that scholars also were attracted to the place. On the political side, there were whole big families such as ours and also the Malaviya family who were politically involved. And above all, of course, a very big religious centre; it has been a place of pilgrimage for hundreds of years. My own recollection is much more of the political side actually because I was too small to be involved in any of the others, except that I do remember going to the Ganges with my grandmother and visiting various temples on its banks.

*   *   *

The Indian National Congress already had a long history. My father had returned from England in 1912 and Gandhiji had come back in 1915 after twenty-one years in South Africa where the mistreatment of the Indians had led him to organise a campaign of non-violent passive resistance against General Smuts' government. To this movement he gave the name "Satyagraha", a Sanskrit word meaning "truth force" or "holding firmly to the truth".

During World War I, Gandhiji had avoided controversial policies and had been active in aiding the Allies by recruiting an ambulance unit. But, in 1919, the passage of the Rowlatt Act aroused his determination to oppose the British policy of repression. He started a Satyagraha Sabha and appealed to the people to join it. Its members were pledged to disobey unjust laws and to court arrests for civil disobedience.

On 13 April 1919, the Punjabi new year's day, took place the massacre of Jallianwalla Bagh which could be described as the most infamous atrocity in the annals of the British Rule in India. At a public meeting organised by the Congress Party in Amritsar, one of the chief towns of the Punjab province, an enormous and peaceful crowd of about 20,000 people — men, women and children — was sealed off in an enclosed space and fired upon by the British troops.

It is very difficult for me to pinpoint whether I actually heard about Jallianwalla Bagh, but I was very conscious that something had happened which was causing excitement in the family and amongst our many visitors. Later on, of course, I heard about it in detail and that was the turning point, not only for our family but for many in India who until then had been taking a far more moderate view of the fight with the British.

At first there was no definite news. Martial Law drew a curtain around Punjab, allowing only frightening rumours to leak through. But gradually the full horror of the holocaust unfolded.[1]

I still remember the national songs of those days calling for revenge. A young Punjabi waited for twenty years to shoot Sir Michael O' Dwyer, the then Lieutenant Governor. But the answer which Gandhiji wanted us to give was of a different kind. Jallianwala Bagh could not be avenged by the taking of lives but only by the ending of imperialism itself.

---

1. According to the official British Committee's report, 379 persons were killed and 1,200 wounded. Later, Brigadier Dyer, who had opened the firing, callously told the Committee that he stopped firing only because his stock of ammunitions had run out after 1,650 rounds.

Jallianwala Bagh was a turning point in our history. It gave a new quality and a new dimension to our national struggle. A movement which had been largely confined to intellectuals spread rapidly to all sections of the masses and to all parts of the land. Hesitation and doubt were swept aside.

These millions of unknown men, women and children to whom Tagore[1] referred were the heroes of the struggle for freedom. And as they and many others fell, thousands arose in their place. The tide of the movement surged forward and overwhelmed the great imperial power. Thus we wrested our freedom. This is when the family came much closer to Mahatma Gandhi and our whole way of life changed from then onwards.

* * *

In December the same year, my grandfather Pandit Motilal Nehru was elected President of the Amritsar session. He was a "grand seigneur". He was not a very tall man, now that I think of it, but somehow he appeared to be tall and broad. He certainly dominated any room or any scene where he was present. Most people, including my father, were frightened of his temper. Yet I was not. I don't think he ever displayed his temper before me. I remember him more for his laughter; it was so infectious. Not only did the whole house — and it was an enormous house — resound with it, but everybody automatically joined in, even the most morose people. He did everything in a big way. When he was earning a great deal, he was spending a great deal. He believed in good living. It didn't worry him to abandon that life for an almost overnight change. He was more concerned with the suffering that my father would have to undergo, than by a mere change of style for himself or the family.

* * *

---

1. Rabindranath Tagore returned the knighthood which had been conferred upon him by the British, with these words: "The very least I can do for my country is to take all consequences upon myself in giving voice to this protest of the millions of my countrymen, surprised into a dumb anguish of terror. The time has come when badges of honour make our shame glaring in their incongruous context of humiliation."

In the autumn of 1920, the Indian National Congress, meeting in a special session, passed a resolution accepting Gandhiji's policy of non-cooperation. The programme included the boycott of titles, of government owned or aided schools and colleges, of law courts, of legislatures, and of foreign goods. It advocated resistance to unjust laws and willingness to suffer imprisonment peacefully. Thus Gandhiji's policy of Satyagraha became the Congress policy. In November 1921, Gandhiji proclaimed a nationwide *hartal* on the occasion of the Prince of Wales' visit. The Government decided to strike at the Congress and members of our family were among the first to be arrested. I saw my father pay frequent visits to jail and, before I was 13, he had been convicted and sentenced five times. All this in fact amounted to a suspension of normal family life and a highly charged and tense atmosphere. And although prison-going was a matter of pride for us, it was very disturbing to the family. Later, one got more used to it.

The tension was not only due to prison terms, but when my parents were fined they didn't pay the fine[1], it was a policy, so the police used to come and take any bit of property in lieu of the fine and quite often — in fact always — they took much more than the fine. If the fine was 500 rupees, they would take a carpet worth thousands or a car or something like that. Then there used to be searches for seditious literature and so on.

At this point there was also tension within the family, because some relatives didn't approve of my parents being so much involved. They felt that perhaps my grandfather wouldn't have been involved if my father wasn't; and also that my mother influenced my father, and that if she had stood out, he would also have hesitated. I doubt if he would have.

So not only was I worried about the British and the police but also about this spoken and unspoken criticism of my parents, and from a very early age I became rather independent. I felt that rather than

---

1. In his autobiography, Nehru notes: "It was the Congress policy not to pay fines. So the police came day after day and attached and carried away bits of furniture. Indira, my four-year-old daughter, was greatly annoyed at this continuous process of despoliation and protested to the police and expressed her strong displeasure. I am afraid those early impressions are likely to colour her future views about the police force generally."

relying on my parents, it was my business to protect them from all this as far as I could.

*   *   *

My education suffered not because of my parents being in prison, but because the type of school to which I could go seemed so remote from the life we had at home that I just wasn't in a mood to take in anything from them. It just seemed to me that what they were trying to teach had nothing to do with life, and when a child is not interested he shuts his mind. I think that was because at that time I was going to an English school. Also, we wore *khadi* and in those days, it was extremely thick. Almost like sack-cloth. The children and everybody else at school were dressed in other types of clothes — you know a child likes to conform, he doesn't like to be different — so I developed a resistance to the school.

I was fascinated by Joan of Arc because she fought the British, and because being a girl, she seemed closer to me than other freedom fighters. I was fascinated by anything to do with the freedom of any country. My father had introduced me to stories of Garibaldi in Italy, Bolivar in South America, and so on. This was the sort of person I liked reading about best.

One of the books that made a deep impression on me was *Les Miserables*, which I read in French by the way. It was so vivid in my mind that for a long time afterwards, until I was quite grown up, I could still visualise the various scenes in it. I think it also had an influence on my social philosophy, it made poverty more vivid to me.

*   *   *

In March 1926, I went to Geneva with my parents and joined L 'Ecole Internationale. It was my first contact with Europe. I did not know a word of French and I knew very little English when I arrived. My father went off and left me in a flat with my mother who was not well. I had to deal with the maid, order the food and so on. This is how I learnt French — the hard way or may be the easiest. I had to go to the market and point things out and then the merchants would tell me what they were called. I don't know how all this affected me. I knew I was in a different country and a different environment, but I had been so used to meeting Europeans that I was not conscious of people around me being of a different race or language and I took it as a matter of course. It helped me become more independent because, as I said, I was more or less in charge of the household. My aunt was there but I think she used to go with my father to various places. Later, I left the Ecole Internationale for the Ecole Nouvelle in Bex. I enjoyed both these schools very much. I not only enjoyed them but kept in touch with them. The Principal of the Bex school died last year, just two months short her 100th birthday. She was writing to me right up to a month before — right up to when she fell ill. I met her when I went to Paris. People from the International School still write to me occasionally.

Even as a small child, I was very keen on nature. At the International School they attached great importance to the study of nature: we studied leaves, insects and everything in detail. I think that also had a life-long influence.

* * *

We returned to India for the Madras Congress in 1927. We came to Ceylon by ship from Marseilles to Colombo. Then we went straight to Madras to attend the Congress and we travelled about in South India.

Like all children I suppose I asked a great many questions and, like all parents, my father chose which ones he should reply to. One of the questions was about the beginnings of the world and man and so on. This is when my father decided to write me a series of letters which were later published as *Letters from a Father to a Daughter*. He started writing them in 1928, while my mother and I were in Mussoorie, and later followed them up with a correspondence course in world history written in jail and published under the title *Glimpses of World History*. Whenever he was at home he usually spent time talking to me. When I asked questions, he would of his own choose to tell me things which he thought I should know about. Much of this was above my head: some things I retained and a lot I forgot.

The same happened with books. I read a lot of books which I couldn't possibly understand. And long afterwards I realised that what I had construed in a very simplistic way was something quite different. In the same way, the letters were a follow-up of our talks.

I think my father was aware that the education one got in schools was very inadequate. For his part, my grandfather didn't believe in that sort of education at all. So, usually I spent the summer in the hills which meant that I missed a lot of the school period, I would arrive in mid-term when they had started new subjects. Some of them — such as history — I could catch up with by reading. But geometry is something different: you don't even know what it means when you arrive in the middle of the course. But my grandfather's general attitude was that it just didn't matter whether you passed or failed. This is why my father was really educating me through his letters and through his talks.

*   *   *

Compared to other children, I guess my father took me quite seriously. I remember him as being quite stern especially in my early years. But I loved both my parents very deeply and they had a considerable influence on me.

Sometimes we used to read together, I mean the whole family. Either we read plays, each person taking a different part, or we read books, each person reading a different chapter.

Most evenings, when my father was home, there was a little time when my mother and he used to read the *Ramayana* or something like that. He was always very keen on Sanskrit and my mother was learning it.

My father also believed in physical exercise and in keeping fit, so I had to run every day, and not just run but run with style. He said it didn't matter whether I ran a long distance or not, but I must be graceful while running. Similarly, he was very anxious that I should know how to swim; his method of teaching was simply to push me in and then let me try to get out as well as I could. I did a little riding, but not much, because by that time we had got rid of our horses. And when I was in Europe, of course, we went skiing. I kept up swimming until a few years ago.

At the Convent School in Allahabad, I was unhappy, and I didn't learn anything because most of the girls there were Anglo-Indians and very pro-British. We were always being scolded, although the nuns themselves — who were of German and other nationalities, not British — were quite sympathetic. But the Anglo-Indian teachers were very critical of the way in which I used to take part in processions: if I participated in an Indian festival — such as Holi, the festival of colours — they would say that it was a barbarian custom. So I was unhappy and spent a lot of time standing on the bench. There was also this problem of my not going to school at the right time, of being sent off to the hills even when the rest of the family could not.

In 1930 I think they were all in prison, and my grandfather insisted that I should go somewhere. So, I went to Nainital, because some distant relative was living there. Although I kept saying "I will be miserable there because I don't know anybody," my grandfather felt very strongly that I shouldn't be in the heat. Then my father, who wanted to send me to Santiniketan wrote to Mr. Vakil who had been in Cambridge with him and was teaching English Literature there, to ask what he thought of the idea. Mr. Vakil wrote back that I could go to Santiniketan after finishing school. But he didn't approve of my going to school there. He himself had a school but it was only a kindergarten and by then, of course, I was too old. But, he said, if you send her to Poona I will tutor her and look after her. At that time, I was absolutely alone in the house, but for my grandmother's sister whom I didn't like at all for some reason. In fact I should say that I hated her — with all the capacity for hatred that a child can have because I thought she was against my parents. She didn't approve of them. So, when I was consulted, I said yes. I would try going to Poona. But I only went there after my grandfather died.

*   *   *

Before that, I had got involved in politics. I can't remember the date, but Mridula Sarabhai, a Congresswoman and a family friend, told me that I was only about 7, 8 or 9, when I formed the children's spinning group. I had asked Gandhiji how I could contribute to our struggle, and he suggested it. It was called Bal-Charkha Sangh and was in fact a children's section of the Gandhi Charkha Sangh, an organisation for hand-spinning; but so far as I can remember we didn't have charkhas, we had *taklis*. Until quite recently in fact, I still had a horribly thick handkerchief which I had spun and woven myself, and then sewn up afterwards. But now it is lost.

Then, of course, I was much more involved in the 1930 movement, because I was old enough to understand what it was all about. I wanted to join the Congress Party and be a regular soldier of India, as my father said. But I was told I was too young to join, so, what was known as Vanar Sena (named after a story in the old Hindu epic, *Ramayana*) or Monkey Brigade was formed. It performed a number of functions, rather like what women did in World War I: everything that would relieve the men. For us, it was not a matter of relieving just the men, but all grown-ups. Sewing and hanging national flags, cooking food for people who were marching, serving water and things to people in meetings or rallies, writing letters for prisoners who didn't know how to write, giving first aid to Congress volunteers, injured in the police *lathi* charges.

Once, firing broke out in a village not far from our home. But, in those days (1929-31), even when people were severely injured, no doctor would come and treat them. The doctor would wait until it was dark, until nobody could see that he was coming and report him to the government. So, we had to go ourselves to these wounded young boys — most of them were between 14 and 17 — and we turned a large room of our house into a hospital ward. This was my introduction to service. I was 13 or 14 at the time.

In the Monkey Brigade, we also had our own meetings and processions. But, of course, it is a minor thing that most foreigners seem to have noticed about our movement: among us were a lot of poor children who used to play in the streets of the city, and they often picked up information about who was going to be arrested or whose house was about to be raided. So we usually knew beforehand, and we could convey it to the people concerned; although we hadn't started the movement with anything like this in view. People treated it as a big joke when it started, but they ended up taking us quite seriously because we really did contribute to the struggle. The movement had branches in other cities, like Bombay for instance. But they were independent, other people started them. And, of course, we joined in some of the grown-up activities like when they were making salt.[1]

1929 was a crucial year for the independence movement. The Congress met in Lahore and elected my father President. It also adopted Purna Swaraj (complete independence) as its goal. The resolution was drafted by my father. I remember when it was being typed by his secretary, I was reading it aloud to my father who drafted it. I mean, I was trying to read it. My father said:

Read it properly.

So, I read it out aloud and then he said:

Well, now that you have read it, you also are committed to it!

And I understood this much better than all the talk about Dominion Status and so on. This thing of being completely free made sense to me.

I also remember my father's presidentship of the Congress and our stay in Lahore quite clearly. It was bitterly cold and we all stayed in tents. As the Congress President, he led the procession and went on a white horse. We were standing, my grandmother and all the family, in a shop or in somebody's house, on the first floor, so that we could get a good view. Close by, there was a band playing a tune, the one they knew best and they played "God save the King!"

*   *   *

After my grandfather died, my parents and I went to Ceylon. We were there about a month. We toured all over the island. I think we visited every historic site. My father had told me a great deal about Buddha before we went. The island was very lush, green and beautiful.

---

1. Gandhi had called on the people to offer Satyagraha by breaking the salt laws. The State salt monopoly prohibited the collection of salt from seawater. On 12 March 1930, he began a march on foot to Dandi, a small seacoast village about two hundred miles from Ahmedabad where he was to break the law. Thousands joined him on the way. On their arrival at Dandi in early April, they spent the night in prayer. In the morning, Gandhi entered the sea to collect water, from which he then extracted salt. Throughout the country, people began to make salt in evaporation pans.

Then we toured South India and that was also a new experience because the life-style there was quite different. Although I had been to villages with my parents, we had never lived in one, except in the day-time, or we may have just spent a night and gone away. But, in South India we spent all our time in small towns, living with very orthodox families and had to wash at the wells.

Although it was a private visit, my father was a leader of the Congress, and we had tremendous crowds. We wouldn't sleep a wink at night. There was no gap between anything; we stayed up all night. When we arrived, all we could do was to have a quick bath and the programme started.

At home, I had never been aware of caste, or anything like that, because there was no occasion to feel that someone was an untouchable. We had had untouchable servants from the very beginning. For instance, my grandfather's own servant, Hari, was an untouchable and he was like one of the family; he sometimes ate with us. But in the South, it was much stricter than in the North, and for the first time, the injustice of it came to me: there were whole streets where untouchables could not walk, which were reserved to "Brahmins only". We said Hari was a Brahmin and he went everywhere with us so it didn't affect us.

But I became conscious of this through small incidents. In Kerala for instance, the custom was that the first son of a Namboodri brahmin married a Namboodri brahmin, but the second son would marry a lower brahmin. Then the second son couldn't eat with his wife and children because they were of a lower sub-caste. We stayed in a family where everybody ate together; as we were leaving for the next town where we were going to meet his father, our host said:

> Look, don't tell my father that we were all eating together because he will be horrified.

On the same visit my mother also made a speech. She was a convinced feminist, a position which I didn't understand then because I felt that I could do what I liked and that it didn't make any difference whether I was a boy or a girl. In her childhood, my mother had felt the disadvantages of being a girl and being forbidden to do many things which a boy could do.

So in Hyderabad she spoke to women about coming out of purdah and many of them did. My father received indignant letters from their husbands saying: "Your wife has been provoking our women."

* * *

In 1930 the mass civil disobedience movement had come to a peak. My mother was actively involved in city politics. I remember vividly when, on 1 January 1931, she was arrested. We were having dinner when a phone call came. I went to take it and it was a warning: they just said that Mrs. Nehru would be arrested the next morning. Before I could reply they put down the phone and we didn't find out who called. I went and told her. She said a lot had to be done before her arrest. She called a meeting of prominent Congress workers and, in the meantime, she asked me to pack for her. Since she thought the house might also be searched, we had to get rid of certain papers. This was New Year's Eve and I remember that at midnight precisely we all read out Tennyson's poem "Ring out the old and bring in the new." She was arrested at about 5 a.m. My own feelings were mixed. I was unhappy about her going, but I was happy because she also wanted it so much.

When I was studying at the Convent, and during the days of the Salt Satyagraha, there was a flag-hoisting in a place where Feroze[1] was studying. I think that is where he saw me first. Somebody else was doing the flag-hoisting. I had just gone along but then there was a *lathi* charge and the person who was hoisting the flag was arrested. He gave me the flag and said:

Don't let it fall.

I was terribly excited and tense but I was very proud. Even though I fell and was hurt, I didn't allow the flag to fall. Somebody took it from me after that. That was my first experience of *lathi.*

* * *

---

1. Feroze Gandhi, who later became my husband.

Then came the Poona school. It was while my mother was in prison that my father started worrying about my being alone in the house. In between, my grandfather died in Lucknow, and the body was brought from Lucknow. This was my first close contact with death.

1932 marked the end of the Round Table Conference and the resumption of civil disobedience. Gandhi, my father and other leaders were in prison again. On 18 September, Mahatma Gandhi started a "fast unto death"[1] and I went to meet him in Yeravada prison in Poona. He looked very weak. But he managed to notice that I had put on some weight. He sent a telegram to my father saying:

"Indu is in possession of more flesh."

In this school I was very active. When I arrived, it was called the Children's Own School and it was just a kindergarten because its founders, Mrs. Vakil's own daughters, were still rather small. After I came though, a lot of people wanted to send their children and, almost overnight, it blossomed into a full school, right up to the matric class. Then we, the children ourselves, decided to change the name from the Children's Own School to Pupils' Own School.

I was secretary of the Literary Society. When Gandhiji undertook his fast we used to go to a sweepers' colony and not only sweep the streets and houses but also wash the children. We adopted two girls. One of them went back. We kept one. The school contributed free education and we paid for clothes and food: Every morning I used to bathe and dress the girl.

The Poona school prepared me for Santiniketan because both the Vakils had lived and worked there for many years. Mrs. Vakil was steeped in the Santiniketan atmosphere, so the teaching as well as the cultural activities of the Poona school were all based on the Santiniketan model and we had our lessons outdoors.

Mrs. Vakil was a talented singer even before going to Santiniketan. There she took an interest in decorative arts. She became expert in making flower jewellery and flower decorations which Tagore had admired in Tripura. He had also brought batik from Indonesia. I think

---

1. In protest against the British government's communal award granting a separate electorate to the depressed classes of India. This social injustice, which the British were trying to make into a permanent political tact, aroused the people and led to a tremendous upheaval.

that, although there had been batik work in India, we had lost the skill. Santiniketan revived it, and a lot of batik work was done there. Mrs. Vakil was good at it and she taught it in the Poona school. In fact, when we had moved to Bombay, she had engaged a Bengali teacher for Manipuri dancing and I started learning to dance there and took part in a school dance drama. We also learnt several Santiniketan songs. When Tagore brought his troupe to Bombay, we went to every single show, not just to watch and learn, but also to help with various odd jobs.

In Poona the school was located in a small house. Life was austere there. In the daytime it was a school and at night hostel and home. At night beds were put in what became class-rooms during the day. In the mornings we had to take them away and prepare the rooms for classes.

Then plague broke out in Poona and all schools had to close. They stayed closed for a while and, rather than have us miss a year, the whole school — well, those who could — went to Bombay. This is how I passed my matriculation exam in Bombay, in April 1934.

*   *   *

I was sixteen and my success was greeted by the not unusual occurrence of my father's arrest. He sent a telegram:

"Going to other home."

I can't say that I was very happy about the exam. I had inherited my grandfather's attitude: naturally I didn't want to fail, but it didn't bother me too much.

After I passed, I went to Kashmir for the summer holidays. That was my first visit to Kashmir, and I thought it was the most beautiful place I had ever seen.

I was there with my uncle and aunt, Mr. and Mrs. Pandit, and their family. Mr. Pandit was then translating Kalhana's *Rajatarangini* (The River of Kings), an eleventh century history of Kashmir (which had earlier been translated by Aurel Stein[1]). So, he was mostly interested in visiting the historic places; this was very interesting for me also.

---

1. M. A. Stein: *Chronicle of the Kings of Kashmir.* English translation of the *Rajatarangini.*

Then I went to Calcutta to be with my mother and to share with her the unsatisfactory but greatly treasured 20-minute fortnightly interview with my father. Mummy and I spent much time at the Ramakrishna Math.[1] Sitting peacefully by the riverside, a new world of thought and experience opened out to me.

*   *   *

Soon afterwards, I joined Vishwa Bharati in Santiniketan. My mother took me there. I think both my parents had visited it before, but I can't remember whether my father accompanied us when I enrolled as a student.

As I said earlier, the Poona school prepared me for Santiniketan. Thus, when I went to Santiniketan it was easier to fit in. Especially since our lives, both in Poona and at home, were very simple. Tagore and all these people were rather surprised. They expected me to be different as I came from a rich home.

At Santiniketan we had to get up at four in the morning and wash our clothes and clean our rooms. Although I was a college student I also joined the Arts Section and did painting as well as dancing. We had the opportunity of being very close to Tagore who took a great deal of interest in the girls and in the arts especially. Quite often he used to just walk around to see what we were doing. Often our dancing classes were held in his own house so that he could watch.

I was rather overawed by Gurudev Tagore's magnificent presence. Never would I dare to encroach upon his time, had he himself not complained of negligence. He kept close watch on all cross currents in the institution. Many were the evenings when a small group of us sat at his feet and talked on diverse subjects, or silently watched him paint. Often he would recite or read aloud. These were moments of serene joy, memories to cherish.

Gurudev was himself part of all time. He conversed with the sages of our civilisation, yet he walked in the modern age. He combined the eternal and the immediate. He reconciled the universal with the local. That is why he gave the name Vishwa Bharati to this great school. He wanted every university student to become a *vishwa-manava*, a

---

1. Headquarters of the Ramakrishna Mission at Belur near Calcutta.

universal individual, who knew no narrowness and who could say: "The world is my home and all men are my brothers."

But even the universal has to find an identity of place and nationality, to find a local form and name. That is why the poet was proud of being an Indian while aspiring to be a universal man. My father expressed the same idea in a different way when he declared that no one could be truly international unless he also was intensely national. It was true of both Gurudev and my father; neither of them could think of realising the universal by escaping from his Indian identity. The Poet spoke once of finding freedom in a thousand bonds of delight. A thousand bonds of delight linked him to his motherland. His creed was one of affirmation. His greatest dreams were dreamt for his country and for his fellowmen.

Gurudev Tagore was certainly a great poet. But he was also something bigger. Poetry was only one part of him. He was a very great human being and it was our great privilege to have him as a fellow Indian. It would not be right for us to claim that he belonged to India only. He left his mark wherever he went. He was a symbol of what we regard as Indian culture and of the values which have come down to us through the ages. In fact, I think, although many other great Indians have also supported these values and have put them into modern language to make them more comprehensible to the ordinary man, it was Gurudev who was able to give the clearest articulation and the greatest cohesion to them. All of Gurudev's ideas, poems and prayers were concerned not with any narrow culture but with, for instance, freedom — freedom not merely in the political sense but freedom from ignorance, freedom from superstition, freedom from bigotry and narrowness. All his ideas and attempts were to lift the human being to a higher level.

Santiniketan lived up to its name as it had a peaceful atmosphere. It was a house of the arts. Something of this I had experienced in Poona earlier. My father had introduced me to poetry, but our family was rather unmusical (incidentally, it was Feroze who introduced me to Western classical music), so I had not heard much music before I went to Poona. Whenever any good musician came (and Poona was a cultural centre of Maharashtra, and attracted well known singers), I would accompany Mrs. Vakil to the recitals. Indian singing takes the whole night because it starts only after dinner and hardly ever ends before next

morning. The Poona school was imbued with an artistic atmosphere
and we did special decorations for our shows (every Saturday) whereas
Santiniketan was totally devoted to the arts and peace.

When I returned to Santiniketan later it had changed greatly.
Some rather ugly buildings have come up. Tagore's radiance was
missing and much of the old atmosphere was lost. There were more
people from other States than there were Bengalis. Also a large
number of foreigners. Students as well as visiting artists and, at that
time, I had a quarrel with Fabri, a Hungarian artist whom I later got
to know well. But he annoyed us in Santiniketan by refusing to take
his shoes off when it was the custom to do so before entering a
particular hall.

There were many interesting and eminent Indian artists like
Nandalal Bose. There was a German Buddhist lama called Gautama.
There were also other foreigners. (In fact, I learnt some German there;
I don't know why, may be someone was teaching German.)

I continued to read books on socialism and politics it seems.
Bernard Shaw's *Intelligent Woman's Guide to Socialism* was noticed in
my room by a visiting British dignitary.

*   *   *

I spent one academic year in Santiniketan[1]. In between, I visited my
mother who was ill in the Bhowali Sanatorium (a small station in
wooded mountains near Almora, in the Himalayas). When her
condition worsened, it was decided that she should go to Europe. Her
cousin, Dr. Madan Atal, and I accompanied her. He was a lovable
person though not too practical. All the arrangements and the
bookings were left to me. Even though he talked to the doctors, I also
had to talk to them and find out exactly what had to be done. This is
the same Doctor Atal who first led our medical mission to Spain and
then to China.

---

1. Tagore's letter (April 20, 1935) to her father when Indira left Santiniketan is also
   revealing: "It is with a heavy heart we bade farewell to Indira, for she was such an
   asset to our place. I have watched her very closely and felt admiration for the way
   you have brought her up. I only hope things will turn for the better and she will
   soon return here and get back to her studies."

It is during that period that I got to know about Nazism. Baden Weiler (in the Black Forest, in Germany) was just a village but for our shopping we went to Freiburg and Munich, and we saw how the Jews were being treated. It was obvious.

I had not been brought up to discriminate between race, class or caste, so the whole theory of Aryanism seemed ridiculous to me. After my father came to Baden Weiler, there was a couple in the pension who were very Aryan-looking from Hitler's point of view: tall and very blond, both of them. The man was blind. Everybody used to come and greet us and ask how my mother was. But I felt this couple seemed to be more attentive. One day, when my father was away, the woman came over and said:

> Since my husband is blind, all his senses are much more sensitive. He feels that you are true Aryans and that is why he wants us to be friends with you.

Of course, I was very amused but controlled myself. But my father and I had a good laugh over it.

Mainly because my father felt that just hanging around, being only with sick people, was not good for me, I decided to spend some time at my old school, the Ecole Nouvelle at Bex, in Switzerland.

At about the same time my mother was moved to Lausanne. I was with her when she died. I was only a little over eighteen.

CHAPTER 2

Adolescence

After schooling in Switzerland you went to England and joined Sommerville College at Oxford. Feroze Gandhi, who later became your husband, was then at the London School of Economics. He was an admirer of your mother who had been responsible for enlisting him in the civil disobedience movement as a Congress volunteer.

In March 1941, you returned to India. You had been away for six years, interrupted by two long stays in India. No warm welcome awaited your homecoming. Your father was still in prison and individual civil disobedience had resulted in mass arrests.

M Y MOTHER DIED ON 23 FEBRUARY 1936. SOON afterwards, I joined a school trip to Italy as part of a course on the history of Art. We visited the main cities, museums and so on.

Returning to Bex, the question of the future came up. Should I go to the Sorbonne or to Oxford? My father felt that he knew more people in England. But the decision to go to Oxford was mine eventually. I don't think he had much to do with it.

I started reading for the Oxford exam on my own. I was staying in Bex but not attending school. I was just choosing my own books to study, because people there had no idea of what was wanted at Oxford. I decided to go to England just for the week-end to get advice.

It so happened that Agatha Harrison[1] was having lunch with the Principal of a girls' school. She said: "Miss Baker will know more about it than I do. Why don't you come along?"

I went, and got on very well with Miss Baker who was the Principal of the Badminton School in Bristol. Somehow I have always got on well with my Principals. Miss Baker said that I couldn't possibly continue to study in Bex, and urged me to come to her school. I decided on the spot. Within two hours, I rushed to buy some clothes and I accompanied her to Badminton.

It was at the Badminton School that I took the Oxford exam. But I didn't have much to do with the school itself because I was in what they call the sixth form which is after the secondary curriculum.

However, being there was very interesting. Even in Bex, Mademoiselle Hemmerlin, the Principal, was following developments in India very closely and she read everything she could lay her hands on. She was a friend of Romain Rolland and admirer of Gandhiji.

On our first visit to Switzerland we had met Romain Rolland. I met him again and, after he died, I kept in touch with his sister and Madame Romain Rolland. Mademoiselle Hemmerlin was a real liberal, she believed in the League of Nations. Miss Baker shared these views and she got even more interested in them. I didn't go myself but she was very keen to send her pupils to camps run by the League of Nations or to go to Geneva to study the League.

Both Mademoiselle Hemmerlin and Miss Baker believed in the concept of one world. Miss Baker encouraged us to read books on world affairs and actually the class to which she gave great importance was the one to discuss the week's news. Every Monday morning we discussed the world news so that we had to read the newspapers very carefully to be able to participate intelligently in the discussion. Because I was able to write about Hitler and other contemporary personalities and events with almost a personal experience, it helped my relationship with her. I suppose it also helped later, when following the background given by my father, I took a course on Modern History at Oxford. Although, by that time, with everybody in prison and so on, my heart was not in my studies at all.

---

1. A Quaker, friend of Gandhi and member of the Conciliation Group.

One reason for choosing Oxford was that Feroze was in England. I considered him more as a friend; it was a link with the family and with India. I felt I would be much more cut off in Paris; in England there was far more news about happenings in India.

I had met Feroze in Allahabad when he joined the movement. He became a frequent visitor to our house. He had proposed to me already before I went to Santiniketan, but I had said no. He told my mother about this. Because I had not spoken to my parents, I was very upset that he should have. I was returning from India and Feroze came to join me in Paris. I had gone first, and Feroze joined me there. That's when I finally said yes, on the steps of Montmartre. But we didn't tell anyone.

In London, I soon met many leaders of the Labour Party. Feroze was in touch with both Labour people and Communists. And Krishna Menon[1] had mobilized everybody he could reach for the India League. Agatha Harrison was my guardian; she was supposed to see that I got what I wanted. And Harold Laski[2] was also keeping an eye on me.

*   *   *

I returned to India in 1937 and, with my father, I visited a few countries in South-East Asia. It was my first contact with other Asian people, except for Ceylonese. We went to Burma and Malaysia (it was then the Malay Peninsula which went right down to Singapore). And it was much like India. We got the same sort of tumultuous receptions there as my father got at home. Huge crowds everywhere we went. And, because my mother had just died, and there was talk of a memorial, we received large donations. I remember one experience which was heartening as well as frightening. We had been invited to some ladies' function. My father's programme was so rushed that he had said he couldn't possible go (officially I was the main guest) and had committed himself to some other meeting. But, when they insisted that they would very much have liked him to come, he

---

1. He was running the office of the India League in London, became the first High Commissioner of India in the United Kingdom and then a member of the Nehru Government.

2. Well known Economist.

Indira at Bhowali

Indira's great-grandfather Gangadhar Nehru (left), grandfather Motilal Nehru and father Jawaharlal Nehru (right)

The fort at the Sangam, in Allahabad—the birthplace of Jawaharlal Nehru and Indira Gandhi

Jawaharlal, Kamala and Indira (1918)

Indira, 11, at boarding house in Switzerland

With Mahatma Gandhi in 1935

Indira and other students with Gurudev Rabindranath Tagore at Santiniketan

decided to drop by. They got so excited that they handed him the money which was supposed to be given to me. He just looked in, took the bouquet of flowers and the money and went out. Then, they felt very embarrassed. They didn't know what to do with me. So they decided to organize another collection: the women just came and took off their bangles, their necklaces, anything they had on them, and emptied their purses. I was sitting and it was dropping on my head and on my lap. I was thrilled that they should feel that way, but it was dreadful, all this jewellery falling all over me. Some couldn't get close enough so they would throw their donations from a distance and I had coins hitting me on the head!

* * *

Then I visited some European countries with my father. One of my main concerns in those days was the Spanish Civil War. I felt very strongly about it. But I couldn't go to Spain because I had my exam then. I was very disappointed. I was quite willing to give up the exam and, I think I wrote to my father and said that it was much more important for me to go to Spain than to sit for an exam: I could take the exam later but I could never go to the Spanish war again. But everybody thought it better that I didn't go, so I met my father in Paris when he returned from Spain. There was a conference to which I had gone with him. The Chairman wouldn't let the Passionaria make an address. I was not a delegate or anything, but I got very excited and felt involved, insisting that she should be heard. Finally we held the meeting in some warehouse — a huge empty place. Of course, the Passionaria spoke in Spanish and I didn't understand a word of it, but I could feel the power of her sincerity.

Then we went to Czechoslovakia because my father wanted to visit the Sudetenland. This was in the forefront of the people's mind. A British mission led by Lord Ranciman was staying in the same hotel as us.

We toured all over Czechoslovakia. First to Prague, then to Bratislava and Zlin which was the headquarters of the Bata firm, and the place where the Pilsen beer is made. In most places we were the guests of someone; in Zlin we were Mr. Bata's guests. Czechoslovakia at that time was very depressing. The people were really dreading an attack by Germany any minute and their faces bore a trapped look. Gloom was all over them. It was interesting but a sad experience.

My aunt, Mrs. Pandit, was coming from India and her plane was to land in Budapest. Since we were already in Czechoslovakia, my father suggested that we should go to meet her in Budapest. In between, we had a short holiday in Deauville. I think I caught a chill there because from there we went to Prague and all the time I was in Czechoslovakia. I felt very very tired but I didn't realize I was ill. Everybody remarked that I looked terrible and I was very thin; but because the programme was so full, I just felt I couldn't fall ill. However, when we arrived in Budapest I felt I must sleep, and it was found I had pleurisy; so we were compelled to stay there for a couple of weeks. I didn't see anything. From the hotel I went to an hospital and as soon as I could be moved to another hospital in London.

In February 1939, I joined Sommerville College at Oxford. Then I went back to India for a while with my father. I visited Egypt on the way and returned to England in April. In the summer of 1939 I went to Germany. I didn't really know why. Maybe I just wanted to gauge how things were. Some people sent telegrams warning that war might break out any moment and advising that I should get out of Germany. Then I went to Switzerland. During this whole period — from when I first went to Oxford — I was intensely involved in everything but my studies. This was also the time of the war of China. My father actually was in Chunking in 1939 when war broke out.

*   *   *

Then I returned to London via Spain. It is a long story. First, people told me I would get into trouble in Spain because of my father's visit during the Civil War. This was Franco's Spain and they said one must know some Spanish. Well, I don't know if that was the reason or not, but at the border they really gave us a lot of trouble in the course of which I lost my plane ticket from Lisbon to London. The conditions in Spain were dreadful; there was no food at all. The only people who had food were the Army. When I arrived at the airport and somebody asked me how I enjoyed it (we were just one night in Barcelona), I said I would have enjoyed it more if I had had something to eat. They said: "There is no shortage here, come and have lunch." And I had a delicious lunch at the officers' mess at Barcelona Airport. But in our hotel there was precious little, or the hours for meals were fixed in such a way that we always seemed to miss them.

I stayed one month in Lisbon because I couldn't get a passage to London although everybody was trying to get one for me. They had such a long list that, everyday, we went to the office and we were told: "There is no chance today but come back tomorrow." They wouldn't admit that they just didn't know when there would be a vacant seat. Finally, they said it might be easier to get a ship or a passage by sea. So I sent a telegram saying I would take whatever came first. My friends were really disturbed because nine out of ten ships were being sunk and, in fact, I lost a couple of friends that way. I remember Rani Kichlu, a brilliant Kashmiri physicist. When I left Switzerland, Rani was in Lyon and I had written to her that I had enough money to pay for her passage. If she came to meet me in Lisbon, we could travel together to England. But she was not willing to go. Only when the Germans came did she decide to leave. She travelled by sea and the ship was sunk.

All of them — Dr. Bhandari, Krishna Menon, Feroze — said "We are trying desperately to get an air passage, don't come by sea, no matter what happens; it doesn't matter if you have to stay longer." And they got me a passage. We landed in Bristol and there was an air-raid the night we landed!

I was there during the beginning of the Blitz when there were constant air-raids day and night: dog fights in the daytime and bombings at night. I wanted to do some relief work but nobody was very enthusiastic about enlisting my help. I did get some experience of the situation. I was on a bus once when incendiaries started pouting like rain. I was just in a sari with nothing else. A stretcher-bearer clamped his tin hat on me and said: "What do you think you are doing without a hat?" Naturally, when you are in a situation like this you help out; I didn't believe in going to air-raid shelters because they were overcrowded, smelly and dirty, with everybody doing their business there, especially the children.

* * *

Then I embarked for India. The trip was quite special. We came in a convoy. Some ships were sunk. We were constantly dropping depth charges which shook every bone in one's body and the noise was nerve-racking. It was also my experience with British methods. We experienced humiliation all the way.

We stopped in Cape Town and we were more or less kidnapped by the Indian agent, V. Rama Rao. He gave us a delicious lunch, but we were terribly anxious to see something since we only had one day there. Finally, we did get to see the Parliament.

General Smuts was there at that time. If it wasn't on that particular day, this was around the time when he made that statement about the colour of one's skin being one's passport. Sir V. Rama Rao had directed his driver to show us the town. But we went to the university instead and got hold of some coloured students from whom we asked for introductions in Durban so that we could escape just doing the sights and actually meet people who were involved in the struggle. We were given two addresses in Durban. There, we managed to dodge the Indian community and get off as soon as we were cleared. There were six in our party. They were all Bengalis except for us. We all stepped into one taxi and went straight to one of the addresses — I forget the name now. Feroze volunteered to find out if it was the right place. The woman who came to the door disclaimed all knowledge of the persons we were seeking. But he insisted that we had been given this address only two or three days before. The woman said that we must be mistaken. She kept on looking into the car and saying no. Feroze was obviously arguing with her. Just then the sun came on my face, and as I don't like the sun, I covered my head with my sari. By that time, Feroze had given up and was dejectedly walking back to the car. As I was covering my head she said: "Come back here; where are you from?"

We said: "India."

She replied: "I didn't know."

Feroze was very fair; and she continued: "You know, they are always harassing us and arresting us; but this is the house you are looking for."

So we got down and they took charge of us and showed us around.

Sheila, the English girl married to Ashok Ray, mostly wore saris, but she only had very expensive ones which her mother-in-law had sent for her wedding. She wanted to buy something more simple. When we went to a shop which belonged to an Indian, they recognized us and immediately called Manilal Gandhi.[1] The Indian community wanted to do things for us.

Then we had rather a painful experience. People took it as normal and Dr. Barnard[2] — when I told him about it recently — took it as normal too. But we didn't. Three of us — Feroze, Sheila and I (I was of a much lighter complexion then) — were taken as Europeans, as all the others were darker. In our party nobody was very dark, but on the ship, there was a Gujarati couple whom we met sometimes. They were very dark. In fact, I have never seen such dark Gujaratis. And they had to suffer humiliations all the time. People were rude and nasty to them.

Anyway, the local Indians arranged hotel accommodation for me. I pointed out that I was with a party of friends and that it wasn't nice for me to go and stay in a hotel, that it would be much better if we all stayed on board the ship. They said that they had paid for the room, I could use it or not, as I liked, but the room was mine for one week (we were in Durban for a week). One day we told them that we would go and have a wash in the daytime because the ship was too far away. Once we left in the morning we could only return after dinner. So we went for a wash and while we were there, a page boy came to announce that there was a gentleman to see me. I said: "Could he wait in the lounge, I shall soon be down?"

The man replied that no, he couldn't come into the lounge, as he was an Indian. I asked who did he think we were. He said he didn't care what we were, but that we didn't look Indian so it was all right. We had been allowed to use the room, but the gentleman couldn't come in, he would have to wait in the street. Of course, we washed quickly and rushed downstairs across a small patch of garden, to meet our visitor on the road: it was the person who had paid for the room! We asked him how he could book a room in a place like that, where

---

1. One of the sons of Mahatma Gandhi.
2. Dr. Christian Barnard — the South African heart specialist who acquired international fame by performing the first heart transplant operation in the world.

he, himself, could not get in. It was something we just couldn't swallow. But he took it as natural. He said that, well, he had to put us up in a good hotel. We had many experiences of this kind.

*   *   *

I didn't mention it before. But in England in the days when I was connected with a committee on China, Krishna Menon rang me about a meeting, asking me to help. Would I come down from Oxford? So I did. One was not allowed to leave Oxford; it was breaking rules. At the meeting, to my utter consternation, suddenly he announced that Miss Nehru was going to speak. Before that day I had spoken only at my childhood gatherings, never to a grown-up audience. I was terrified, especially since the hall was so big. It was probably Caxton Hall. I just couldn't get out any sound! Finally, I managed to say something; but there was a drunk in the room who said: "She doesn't speak, she squeaks." This, of course, brought the house down and I vowed that I would never, never speak in public again.

When I arrived in South Africa the Africans said:

We will arrange a reception for you in a hall. We will greet you and then you will speak. ·

I said:

Oh no, I am not going to say a single word, it is only on that condition that I should come.

They were taken aback, because they had booked the hall and made all the arrangements. Eventually, they said that anyway I should sit on the dais and that they would try and explain my silence somehow. All that morning — the reception was at 4 p.m. — I was taken to visit an area where African railway workers lived. The conditions were so terrible that I got worked up. At the reception, when it was announced that Miss Nehru wouldn't speak, I banged the table and said: "I do wish to speak."

The poor chairman was startled, and before he could say anything, I came to the microphone. I don't remember what I said, but I was full of emotion. I must have spoken about the living conditions of the

Bantus and others. It came out in the African papers. The next day, wherever I went, I was mobbed. Women came and kissed me and men shook my hand. Obviously I had said the right things as far as they were concerned.

Whatever the local authorities felt, nothing happened to us. But the local Indians were annoyed because I had told them they were wrong to side with the British.

"You must come to an understanding with the Africans, I had said, because it may not be today, it may be ten or twenty years, but it is they who will rule this country. And then what will your descendants do?"

They didn't approve of this at all. After that they didn't bother about us any more.

* * *

In March 1941 I landed in Bombay. There was no warm welcome for my homecoming. My father was still in prison, and individual civil disobedience had resulted in mass arrests. After having lived in Europe on and off for six years it took me some time to readjust to everything -- the language, the atmosphere, etc. I was met in Bombay by a telegram from Mahatma Gandhi saying that I should first go and see him. I was rather hesitant, but my father also sent a message saying that, since Gandhiji wanted to see me, I should go to Sevagram. I went there and that was also a rather strange experience. Not so far as Gandhiji was concerned, because he was the same as I had known him. But the atmosphere was one of petty quarrels: who would take his food in, who would carry his papers and things like that. Once, the washing was hanging outside and it started raining. So, I ran to take it down, just to help, because I felt I wasn't doing anything. They thought it interference. I hadn't been in the ashram long enough to touch his clothes or anything that belonged to him. In the evening it was even worse. Gandhiji told me to go to the prayer session. There was another girl whom I didn't know, she too was new. We just sat down somewhere. Then we heard some fuss. We didn't realize we were the cause of it until we saw people pointing at us. I got up and asked: "Have we done something wrong?"

They said: "Yes, those places belong to others."

We asked: "Why didn't you say so? We didn't know."

Then this girl and I sat somewhere else. But it was astonishing that such small incidents should be given such importance.

Allahabad was terribly, terribly hot. What struck me most was the heat.

*   *   *

Then I went to Dehra Dun to meet my father. I wasn't too well, with the heat and everything else. He said I should go and stay somewhere in the hills. I wanted to remain in Mussoorie so as to be able to see him. Ultimately I took a cottage and stayed there. When my father was released, we had a Congress Meeting in Bardoli and I accompanied him. Frontier Gandhi[1] and all the leaders were there. By that time, I was back in the swing. I don't know when my father was released. Maybe it was winter. I travelled with him a little while; I think that Sheikh Abdullah was also with us. I cannot remember whether it was before or after Bardoli.

Then I got married. It was just before the Cripps Mission. My marriage was on the 26th of March, and at one time we even thought that my father would not be able to attend it.

---

1. Khan Abdul Gaffar Khan, Nationalist leader of the North-West Frontier Province.

CHAPTER 3

Wife, Mother and Political Leader

Your marriage with Feroze Gandhi "raised a storm." You were breaking some traditions in India because it was an intercommunity marriage.

In May 1942 the "Quit India" slogan was launched by Mahatma Gandhi and the All India Congress Committee meeting in Bombay adopted the historical resolution. On 9 August, Gandhi, Nehru and the entire Congress Committee were arrested. In September of the same year, you were also arrested. Your months in prison must have marked your political coming of age and they have certainly been an important part of your political life.

In 1945 your father was released and the British Cabinet Mission was in India. Mr. Jinnah was determined on the creation of a sovereign Pakistan and the Congress itself was hard pressed to maintain the unity of the sub-continent. This is the period when you were completely a wife and a mother.

On 15 August 1947, India became independent and Mr. Nehru was made Prime Minister. You wrote: "It is one of the proudest and most exciting moments in my life."

When, in September 1947, partition riots broke out in Delhi, you were a enormous help to your father.

On 29 January 1948 you had a last meeting with Mahatma Gandhi: it was on the eve of his death.

FEROZE WAS A PARSI[1]. IN MARRYING HIM I WAS BREAKING age-old traditions. It was an intercommunity and an interreligion marriage. And it did "raise a storm". Yet it was not the first mixed marriage. I received many letters from people who had mixed marriages. But I was perhaps the first person in the public eye to do so. There is no doubt that many people, including my own family, were very upset. Strangely enough, though the person whom I would have expected to be angry — my maternal grandmother — was the one who accepted my marriage most readily.

*   *   *

Immediately after my wedding we had a session of the All India Congress Committee in Allahabad. My husband was in charge of the construction of the *pandal* where the meeting was to be held. And I was put to work with the volunteers. It meant that we had to be out from early morning until late at night and we didn't see each other at all.

We had taken a very small house, but since it was close to the Congress session, they requisitioned half of it for use as an office. We had only two small rooms for ourselves. By this time, it was getting hotter and hotter. My father was going to the Kulu Valley, but Feroze couldn't get away because he had to complete the accounts and sort out other matters. He stayed behind and I went with my father to Kulu. Then, my father returned, Feroze joined me for a trip to Kashmir.

We were Sheikh Abdullah's guests. He wanted us to visit different parts of Kashmir and we did some trekking.

In May, the "Quit India" slogan had been launched by Mahatma Gandhi, and on 9 August Gandhiji, my father and the entire Congress Working Committee were arrested.

In September of the same year I was also arrested. I was working under Mr. Lal Bahadur Shastri. Mr. Shastri, Feroze and a lot of other

---

1. The Parsis are Zoroastrians by religion and believe that Zoroaster brought sacred fire down from heaven. They therefore worship fire, and their temples called fire temples. They originally came to India from Persia, seeking refuge from religious persecution of the Muslim conquerors of the country. There are only about 200,000 Parsis in India today.

people had decided that they would go underground. I remained in the open. I was doing things about literature and money, etc...helping anybody I could, until I heard that I was to be arrested. I sent word to Feroze. He happened to be in Allahabad and felt that there was no point in getting arrested so tamely and that it would be better to organize a meeting at least, because things were quiet at that moment.

*   *   *

Our meeting was banned. The place where the meeting was to be held wasn't given out. We had just said there would be a meeting at such and such an hour and the location was circulated only by word of mouth. The other indications were printed and put out. I went and spent the night somewhere. At the time of the meeting I emerged and, of course, the people knew, for they were scattered in shops, cinemas and so on, and at the right time they all came out. British soldiers were patrolling all the streets not knowing where it would be. This was a sort of square with a cinema on one side. I came out and addressed the gathering. Soon the military came aiming their guns at us. We were surrounded on all sides, and one chap had his bayonet almost touching me. Feroze, who was watching from upstairs, became very excited. He forgot about being underground and he rushed out and said:

Either you shoot or you get away from here.

We were all arrested. Feroze was arrested and so was I. The sergeant made the mistake of touching my arm to lead me to the prison van. It was like a signal. The crowd surged forth, my other arm was grabbed by some Congress woman and I thought I would be torn asunder. But somehow we all survived. There was no firing, though rifle butts were used and many were hurt. The ride to the jail was a rather extraordinary one, for the police in my van were apparently so moved by my talking to them that they apologised, put their turbans at my feet and wept their sorrow because of what their job compelled them to do!

*   *   *

I don't really think that one comes of age politically with one single event. It is a gradual process in which a series of experiences are adding up all the time. Yet, I can certainly say that my months in prison were a very important part of my life.

I had another experience just before being arrested. On 9 August, there was to be a flag-hoisting ceremony presided by the then Congress President. Everybody was going to it — at least all the members of the Working Committee. Maybe it was the regular flag-hoisting of the Congress. So we all went and there, we were teargassed. That was the first time for me.

But prison was a very special sort of experience. Since my earliest childhood, I had visited jails either to go to the trials of relations and friends or for the unsatisfactory but highly treasured 20-minute inter-views with my father. People have heard of my parents' imprisonments but it is not often realized what a large number of relatives, both on my father's and my mother's side — off hand, I can think of two dozen names but there may have been more — spent long years in prison. I do not know of any family which was so involved in the freedom struggle and its hardships.

What a world of difference there is between hearing and seeing from the outside and the actual experience. No one who has not been in prison for any length of time can ever visualize the numbness of spirit that can creep over one when, as Oscar Wilde writes: "Each day is like a year, a year whose days are long." When day after day is wrapped in sameness, spite and deliberate humiliation. As Pethick-Lawrence said: "The essential fact in the life of the prisoner is that he takes on a subhuman status."

Herded together like animals, devoid of dignity of privacy, debarred not only from outside company or news but from all beauty and colour, softness and grace, the ground, the walls, everything around us was mud coloured and so became our jail-washed clothes. Even our food tasted gritty. Through the barred apertures we were exposed to the *loo* (hot summer wind) and dust storms, the monsoon downpour and the winter cold. Others had an interview and letter once or twice a month but not I. My husband was in the same prison. After persistent efforts we were permitted a short interview, but soon he was transferred to another town. I kept cheerful and busy, reading and teaching. I took over the entire care of a small baby whose mother I was coaching to enable her to earn her living on her release.

There was no yearning for the outside world, for no one worthwhile was there. Besides, we had convinced ourselves that we were in for seven years. I was determined to bear all privations and insults smilingly. Many pictures come to mind: the visit of the Civil Surgeon sent by the Governor of the United Provinces, in response to public concern over my ill health. He prescribed a tonic and a special diet including delicacies such as Ovaltine. But hardly had he turned his back when the Superintendent tore up the list and tossed the pieces on the floor.

"If you think you are getting any of this," he said, "you are mistaken." This was surprising for I had not asked for anything — even the surgeon's visit was unexpected.

One night we were startled out of our sleep by a bloodcurdling shriek Although Zohra was the nastiest and most unpopular of our wardresses, we could sympathize with her terror and agitation, for there was an enormous cobra only a yard from our bars, coiled under one of the' clocks which the wardress had to punch on her rounds. So, apart from the imminent danger of a snake-bite, she had the legitimate fear of losing her job. We were locked inside the barrack and she within the outer wall. There was no stick or other weapon. Zohra's shouts, now frightened, now exasperated, now bullying, now entreating did nothing to shake the calm of the sentry outside, who wanted detailed information regarding the exact location of the snake, specification of its length and breadth and so on.

"Are Kambakht!" (Oh, you unfortunate one) shouted Zohra. "Have I got a tailor's tape to measure it from head to tail?"

It was several hours before the sentry could be persuaded to call the matron; her house was three furlongs away and she in turn had to walk to the Superintendent's house to awaken him, before they could go together to the main office to fetch the key to the women's prison. By the time this little procession entered our enclosure, we had long since fallen philosophically asleep and the snake had glided away.

Another day, we barely escaped being burnt to death. It was wartime and the cantonment was crowded with not only British but Americans and Canadians as well. A Canadian ace pilot was smitten by our Superintendent's attractive daughter. Once he was flying low over her house as was his wont, when his wing touched a telegraph wire and burst into flames. We saw it falling towards us at alarming speed but it just skirted the jail wall and dashed into a half-built bungalow not far away.

All things pass and so did this. My unexpected release was like coming suddenly out of a dark passage — I was dazzled with the rush of life, the many hues and textures, the scale of sounds and the range of ideas. Just to touch and listen was a disturbing experience and it took a while to get adjusted to normal living.

* * *

In 1944, my first son was born. My father and I had been exchanging names. I had sent him lists of names and he had done the same. A friend of mine also gave me a list and it included Rajiv. Until then I had never heard of anybody called Rajiv. It means lotus and Kamal, my mother's name also means lotus. My son's real name is Rajiv Ratna. Ratna means the same as Jawahar, so it was a combination of both my parents' names.

One of the reasons I got married was that I was determined to have children, yet I went through a bad time because a doctor had said that I may not survive child-bearing. Unfortunately, he had also put it down in writing. So when I became pregnant there were a lot of misgivings. My doctor in Allahabad refused to take my case because she was also a friend. That is why I went to Bombay and stayed with my aunt. Rajiv was born in Bombay, a perfect baby, with a healthy mother, no labour pains or other trouble.

I think it was one of the most joyful moments in my life, although I must say at that time he seemed quite ugly. Tagore wrote: "Every child comes with the message that God is not discouraged of man."

But to a woman, motherhood is the highest fulfilment. To bring a new being into this world, to see its tiny perfection and to dream of its future greatness is the most moving of all experiences and fills one with wonder and exaltation.

I remember that one day the police had brought my father and Govind Vallabh Pant from Ahmednagar jail to Almora jail or Bareilly jail. They had stopped in Naini jail, in Allahabad, for the night and I had got the message. In fact, we didn't know whether they would stop or not, but we hoped they would and we expected them to be taken off at some wayside station. We had no idea whether my father would actually be taken to Naini prison or if he would just change trains. Feroze and I then took the baby along to show him.

We went to the prison and waited outside. They arrived late at night, because the British always did things in the dark. I lifted the baby up under a very dim roadside light. My father peered at him.

Grandchildren are in a way much more fun than one's own children. Because you don't have the same feeling of responsibility. And also, having gone through the period of your own children, you know that the children are much hardier than you thought when you were very young parents. But I don't think I even got enough time to spend with them. I like playing with them, helping them with their school work and so on. I think the role of a grandmother which I didn't fully have because of the circumstances, is a satisfying one.

*   *   *

In 1945, my father was released. The British Cabinet Mission was in India. Mr. Jinnah was determined to create a sovereign Pakistan and the Congress itself was hard-pressed to maintain the unity of the sub-continent. This is a period when I was nothing but a wife and a mother. I was not very involved and when my father was released, Feroze was in Allahabad but I was actually in Srinagar with the baby. I had taken him to Kashmir because of the summer heat. I remember clearly that I was staying with my uncle (B.K. Nehru's father) who was the Maharaja's Financial Adviser.

The household had all gone to an "at-home", the annual one given by the Maharaja. I was alone in the house. I heard on the radio that my father and others were likely to be released, so I rushed out to book a seat on the bus or train to Allahabad. At that moment, I forgot the baby. When the family returned from the party they wondered how I could help by going. I said: "I don't know but I just have to go."

So I left the baby: there were several relatives and one uncle who was a doctor. Then I returned to Allahabad.

My father went to Bombay, and I accompanied him. There was some meeting where we had to be in the pouring rain for some reason. It was the monsoon period and I caught flu. I couldn't go back until the fever subsided. Then I returned to Kashmir. Soon after, my father came up too. He was there nearly a month. Maulana Azad[1] also came.

Soon after, my father insisted that I join him in Delhi because he was staying with somebody and was not comfortable. While the talks were going on, he asked me to come and look after him. It was a period of strain and political turmoil. In September 1946, my father assumed the leadership of the Interim Government.

*   *   *

Then in December 1946, I gave birth to my second son, Sanjay. The house was full of relatives. Lady Cripps and all kinds of people were there. I was really hoping for a daughter. In fact, we had kept only girls' names ready. My second son's name had to be thought of in a hurry.

Because of the political struggle, my own childhood was an abnormal one, full of loneliness and insecurity. That is why I was determined to devote full time to my children. A child's need of his mother's love and care is as urgent and fundamental as that of a plant for sunshine and water. To a mother, her children must always come first, because they depend on her in a very special way. The main problem in my life was, therefore, how to reconcile my public obligations with my responsibility towards my home and my children.

When Rajiv and Sanjay were babies I did not like the idea of anyone else attending to their needs and I tried to do as much for them as I could. Later when they began school, I was careful to have my engagements during school hours so as to be free when the boys returned home. Once, when Sanjay was quite small, a nursery school friend of his came to our house with his mother. The mother, a society lady of means, commenting on my public work, remarked that I could not be spending much time with my sons. This hurt Sanjay and, before I could think of a reply, he rushed to my rescue with the words:

> My mother does lots of important work, yet she plays with me more than you do with your little boy.

---

1. Maulana Abul Kalam Azad was a prominent Muslim leader of the Congress Party. He became Education Minister in the Nehru Government.

It seemed his little friend had complained about his mother's bridge playing.

However, the amount of time spent with children doesn't matter as much as the manner of spending it. When one has only a limited period of time at one's disposal, one naturally makes the most of it. No matter how busy I have been, how tired, or even unwell, I have always taken time off to play or read with my sons.

One can teach best by example. Children are extraordinarily perceptive and quick to detect any falsehood or pretence. If they trust and respect you, they will co-operate with you even at a very young age. My elder son, Rajiv, had been a happy laughing baby but at the age of three, the advent of a baby brother coinciding with our move from the familiar Allahabad atmosphere and many other changes upset him. I was far from well and I found his tantrums very irritating. Scolding him only made it worse. So I tried reasoning. I told him that much as I loved him, his shouting disturbed me.

"What can I do?" he said, "I don't want to cry, it just comes."

I said: "There is a nice fountain in our garden. When you want to cry or shout, go to the fountain and do it there."

After that, at the first sign of tears, I would whisper "fountain" and away he went. In the garden there was much to distract his attention and he soon forgot his troubles.

As the boys grew older, they went to boarding school. That is when I began touring the country. I would travel extensively while they were away, so as to be with them during the holidays. Whenever I was separated from the boys I wrote to them at least once a week and sometimes oftener, so that they would know that I was thinking of them.

Life is a mixture of happiness and sorrow. Education in the widest sense of the word is the training of the mind and body, so as to produce a balanced personality which is capable of adjusting, without undue disturbance, to life's changing situations. This cannot be achieved through schools or book knowledge alone. Much of the burden falls on the mother, who must help the child develop self-discipline and strengthen his character. Real love is not that which gives in to the child's whims but which can also discipline and teach whenever necessary.

Rajiv was under 12 years old when he had to have an operation. The surgeon wanted to tell him that it would not hurt, but in my opinion this would have been an insult to the child's intelligence, so I interrupted him to inform Rajiv that there would be considerable pain and discomfort for a few days after the operation. Had it been possible for me to take on his suffering I should gladly have done so, but since this was not possible, he must be prepared to endure it. Weeping or complaining would make no difference except perhaps to produce a headache as well. Rajiv never once cried out or con ned he bore the pains smilingly. The doctor said he had never h   uch a good patient even among older people.

My public work sometimes took me away from the children. Yet even they have felt it worthwhile because through it I am attempting to play my part in building a better future for all the children of India.

Even in more advanced countries, recognition of the individuality of the child and of his special rights is comparatively recent. It has come about through trials and errors, and through the consciousness that a lack of this recognition and of the action necessary to support it, creates grave problems for society.

Since the advent of the industrial revolution the momentum of our lives is becoming faster inexorably. The struggle for existence, for earning a living, for finding "a place in the sun" as they say, involves increasing mental strain.

To keep abreast of events, one has constantly to adjust oneself to changing conditions. This naturally is more difficult as one grows older. The result is an ever-widening gulf between the thinking of one generation and that of the next.

Khalil Gibran, the famous poet-philosopher writes of children:

> *You may give them your love but*
> *not your thoughts,*
> *For they have their own thoughts.*
> *You may house their bodies but*
> *not their souls,*
> *For their souls dwell in the house*
> *of tomorrow, which you cannot visit,*
> *not even in your dreams.*

* * *

How many parents are aware of the gaping chasm? Most people see their children as extensions of themselves, and want to use them for the fulfilment of their own thwarted ambitions.

Sometimes this means that out of love and respect for his parents, the emerging adult has to stifle his own desires and inclinations, he has to surrender his chosen field, for which he may have a special affinity and aptitude, to that of his parents or guardian's wishes.

Often enough this struggle deadens his enthusiasm and his *joie de vivre* and society has yet one more cog in the machine existing dully instead of an individual living vibrantly and radiantly, giving himself wholeheartedly to his work and play and serving the community.

What mother would not gladly take on the sufferings of her child, if only she could? But, alas, we learn soon enough that "in the last resort we are neither father nor mother, neither husband nor wife nor child, we are each a private and lonely universe, we must each live in the truth of our own law, our own quality."

Should the parents then be mere bystanders and allow the child to go his own sweet way, unchecked and unshepherded? No, life isn't as easy as that! We parents have the exceedingly complex and delicate task of guiding unobtrusively, without yielding to the temptation of imprinting on the child our own personality or imposing on him our own desires.

We have to give him courage and self confidence and to help him develop, as Mr. Smith, the Master of Balliol College at Oxford, wrote to the Prime Minister of England in 1919:

An open habit of mind, clear-sighted and truth-loving is proof against sophisms, shibboleths, claptrap phrases and cant.

If this were our aim, we would be giving our children a solid foundation for successful living and deep security which the present effort of merely securing soft jobs for them can never achieve.

* * *

On 15 August 1947, India became independent and my father was made Prime Minister. Somewhere I wrote:

It is one of the proudest and most exciting moments in my life.

It was the culmination which so many people had fought for. Yet, when it actually came, I think one was more numbed than anything. When you feel something very intensely, you can hardly feel it. You are not sure whether it has happened or not.

In September 1947, partition riots broke out in Delhi. I was in Mussoorie. I had taken the children up and I used to come up and down in my small car. As the children were up in Mussoorie I stayed there for a while. Delhi phoned saying: "Don't come back just yet."

I thought it may be because of the heat. No more news, and I couldn't get through to the house. Every time I tried to send a message, all I got back was: "Don't come home."

I was highly suspicious. I didn't know what was happening. Finally, when I got through to Feroze, who was with my father, he said: "Well, apart from everything else we haven't got much to eat and you can't bring the children."

I said: "I shall bring lots of potatoes and everybody can live on potatoes."

He said that the situation was dangerous. I said: "Well, if it is dangerous, that is one more reason why I should be there rather than sitting here on my own." So, I packed up and came down the same evening, bringing as many potatoes as I could — two sacks full I think.

When we arrived in Dehra Dun we heard that there had just been a riot. Then, in Shahdara or somewhere between there and Delhi, the train stopped where it was not supposed to stop. I was actually washing — because Indian trains are pretty dirty with the coal — as we were about to arrive. I looked out to see why the train had stopped and I found people chasing somebody. I got off and tried to control the situation. I did manage to save one man, but another was too far away and there were too many people chasing him.

I was merely dressed in a towel so I couldn't do anything. Then, I got home and I wasn't at all well. Actually that was one of the reasons for going to Mussoorie. My father advised me to see what was happening in the camps. I started working in the refugee camps along with Mrs. John Mathai. One day on the way home from there, we had a dreadful experience. As we were coming, we saw a man being chased. One solitary man being chased by hundreds of people, a couple of hundreds perhaps. I told the driver: "Stop." But our driver was a Muslim and he dared not. I said: "You have to stop because otherwise I am jumping out." He didn't stop, but he did slow down a bit. I had taken off my chappals because my feet used to swell in the heat. I have never liked the heat and, in those days, I was still very new to it. So, I was barefoot. I just got out of the car, went up to the crowd and got hold of the man they were chasing and put him behind me.

"What do you think you are doing?" they asked.

"I am saving this man's life; you can only kill him after you have killed me."

They didn't know who I was. They said: " Do you think we can't kill you?"

I said: "Anybody can kill me, but you are not going to, you don't have the courage and you are not going to."

I was telling this wretched man to run to the car and holding off the people; but he was hung on to my sari and wouldn't let go, so we kept stepping backwards. As I faced up to them, they didn't do anything. They looked threatening, but they didn't do anything. Then we brought the man to the car. We took him straight to hospital; he was badly hurt on the head, but he survived.

Somehow Gandhiji heard about this. I certainly didn't tell anybody, not even my father. But Gandhiji heard about it. We used to go every evening to see him, just before prayer time, and one day a phone call came to ask whether we were coming or not. We went. Gandhiji asked: "I have heard about this Shahdara incident, is it true?"

"It is true," I said.

"Why didn't you tell me?" he asked.

I replied: "I didn't think it was anything special to tell you because I just acted on reflex. Sometimes one has to do something without thinking. May be if one thought of the danger, one would hesitate, but the feeling that this has to be done is much stronger than any other thought."

So he asked: "What are you doing?"

I said: "I am going to these camps and it is not a worthwhile work, there are lots of people working and all we do is to dole out things. Anybody can do it."

"It would like somebody to go into the Muslim areas to report to me on the situation there," said Gandhiji.

"Who will go with me?" I asked.

"If I had found anybody to go, I wouldn't ask you because I know that you are not very well," he answered.

I said: "I don't know the city of Delhi and I don't know which are the Muslim areas."

"Just find out!" were his final words.

I asked somebody who would know, because everybody in our house was new to Delhi. Somebody suggested that the Town Hall was the place.

I went to the Town Hall and there I just saw a girl standing. She didn't know who I was and I didn't know who she was. She was wearing a *khadi* sari so I went up to her and asked: "Do you live in Delhi?"

"Yes," she said.

"Do you do any social or political work here?" I asked.

And she said:

"Yes, I work among the labour, the cloth mill people."

I then asked: "Do you know Delhi? Do you know where the Muslim areas are?"

She answered: "Yes."

I said: "Well, this is what Gandhiji has told me. I would like somebody to go with me to Delhi. I'll provide conveyance." She agreed to come with me. Even then, we didn't ask each other's name; we just decided to meet at a particular place.

Then we became absorbed in the work. The Muslims were really in a terrible state. They had no food and nobody could go out. Nothing had been cleaned out for about a month. Because it was the rainy season, some of the streets were full of water with filth floating on it. Sometimes while walking we stepped on a wire and got a shock.

We literally had to clean up the place ourselves. Even when we got hold of a sweeper, he hesitated to enter the locality, afraid of being killed. So we had to have two people standing with him while he was cleaning. There were ration shops but they were empty, so we had to go ourselves to get the rations.

The attitude of the officials was also "communal." At first, they said that there was nothing to spare and that obviously Muslims couldn't have the first choice. We said that it was not a question of first or second choice. They were Indian citizens and we were not responsible for whatever was happening in Pakistan. We could not allow them to die of starvation or illness, as we had accepted partition. Then, they would admit there was grain but nothing to carry it in. So we chartered a truck and arranged for the grain to be lifted. I got to know a lot of the boys and people who were working in those areas. We were so busy bringing the grain there. We also took doctors into the locality because of the cholera. This led to a small incident: I was advised to have an anti-cholera injection. Rajkumari Amrit Kaur was then in charge of Health, so I asked her permission. Her reply was that the vaccine could not be wasted. Of course, she didn't know I was working in those areas.

We saved several people from being killed and we also got some who were making trouble arrested. My feud with the R.S.S. started then. Some innocent-looking people walked around with sticks which had swords hidden inside, or a heavy bit of metal, so that if they hit a person, his head would split open.

Suddenly, one day, I said to Subhadra Joshi: "You know, we are getting all these people arrested but where is it taking us? It is not helping the situation. We seem to spend all our time with bad people, through trying to find out who is committing these crimes. It is never-ending, why don't we tackle it in another way? Let us see if there are any people who are not involved in the killing and hatred. Let us try to bring them together."

From then on, we would go into the Muslim areas and say to them: "You know all the people here much better than we do. Are there Hindus who, in spite of all the provocations, remain human?"

They would say: "Yes, so and so."

So we would say: "Suppose we bring those people here."

They said: "No, what would the other people say? We would be boycotted by the community. It would be too dangerous and they would kill us."

We said: "How, if we brought two people here, can they kill all of you?"

Then we would go to the Hindu areas and ask the same question:

"Are there any Muslims here who have not misbehaved no matter what?"

They would say: "Yes, so and so." And we would go backwards.

My father was getting a lot of threatening letters saying: "What does your daughter think she is doing? Our women are being raped there, she will be raped here. We are not going to allow her to do this, she will be killed." All kinds of letters and threats. At one stage, his secretary thought I should have some protection. So instead of the ordinary car which we had been using, we were given a police jeep. A military policeman, with a real sten-gun, used to go with us But he was the only man, apart from the driver of the jeep. Now, when we went into the Muslim areas he used to grab my sari and hide behind me saying: "You have no business going in there, it is very dangerous!'

One day, we were terribly tired because we used to begin at 5.00 in the morning. The car was supposed to pick us up somewhere in the evening, but it wasn't where we expected it and it was quite dark by then. Subhadra said:

"They may have misunderstood and gone to the next crossing. So you sit here, and I will go and look there." We asked the man accompanying us to stay there, so that the two of us could go to see whether the car had come. The man said: "I am not staying alone."

And he had the gun! He said that one of us had to stay there. I don' remember if I or Subhadra stayed back. Somebody did stay in case the car came later. Then we found that the car was stationed somewhere else.

Only after we had brought some cleanliness to the area, arranged for the rations, and got the doctors to go to various places did I go to see Gandhiji again. As nobody had reported to him, he had taken it for granted that I wasn't seeing him because I hadn't done anything about it and I didn't want to face him. When I went, he looked at me sternly and I asked what was the matter. He said: "Didn't I ask you to do something?"

I replied: "Yes, and I have been doing it."

Then I told him what we had done and he asked me why I hadn't come and told him earlier. I said that it seemed more important to get it done than to report on it. Anyhow, we only got back very late.

By then we had started what we called our peace work — going from place to place — finally, we got five Muslims and five Hindus who agreed to meet. It may have been six or seven, but somewhere around that number. They met in fear and trembling, but we said:

"You see, now you've met, nothing has happened, you are all friends, so let's try for a bigger gathering." And we had a bigger gathering. Finally we had a tea party for about 500 people — mixed. I have written about this once, but not in very great detail.

* * *

On 29 January 1948, I had my last meeting with Mahatma Gandhi; it was on the eve of his death. Strangely enough, he had sent for us even on that day. He sent a message reminding us that we hadn't been to see him for some time, though I think "some time" meant only four or five days.

The message came before the prayer meeting. He said if we delayed he would go into prayer and afterwards he had appointments. Miss. Naidu[1] was with us. I took Rajiv along.

My hair was not very long, but I used to do it up as if it were long and the gardener had just brought me flowers to put in it. I said that they were so fragrant that I wouldn't put them in my hair but give them to Gandhiji. We had a very relaxed meeting with him. It was long before prayer, because he was sitting out in the sun with his funny glasses and little hat. Rajiv played with his stoles and we talked about films and all kinds of things like that. The evening before, there had been a film show and my father had asked some of the girls from the ashram to come, but Gandhiji had not allowed them. My father was saying that they were grown-up women and that not allowing them to go was the wrong type of strictness. I went and gave my impression of the film to Gandhiji and he said he was right not to send them. Although by today's standards there was nothing wrong with the film, at that time I thought it had a flavour of vulgarity. Nothing like sex or violence or anything, but I thought there was something about it that was not very nice. So Gandhiji chuckled and

---

1. Daughter of Mrs. Sarojini Naidu, the poet, politician, former President of the Congress and Governor of Uttar Pradesh. A dedicated social and political worker who became Governor of West Bengal.

said to tell my father that he was perfectly right in refusing permission to go.

The next day, we had tea and were just sitting around when we got the news.

*   *   *

Mahatma Gandhi's death was not only a national blow but it was a deep personal pain. He was so much a part of our family and of India that we simply couldn't imagine India without him. He seemed to be the focal point around which everybody in the whole country and the Congress moved. Even when he was not there and meetings were held in his absence, it was such a comfort to know that he was somewhere in the country and that you could reach out to him. I could also understand what it meant to my father, what a void it would become in his life.

Each person's understanding of Gandhiji is a measure of his own change and growth. While he was alive many of my age group found it difficult to understand him. Some of us were impatient with what we considered to be his fads, and we found some of his formulation obscure. We took his Mahatmahood for granted, but quarrelled with him for bringing mysticism into politics. This applied not only to my generation. In his autobiography, my father describes the difficulty which he and others of his generation felt in integrating Gandhian ideas into their own thought structure. But little by little, the experience of the ebb and flow of our national movement enabled my father to arrive at a fuller understanding of Gandhiji and to weave the essential elements of Gandhiji's thinking into his own. He called him a "magician" and devotedly attempted to translate Gandhian thought into contemporary terms, to make it more comprehensible and to extend its influence to young people and intellectuals.

Gandhiji himself did not demand unquestioning obedience. He did not want acceptance of his ends and means without a full examination. He encouraged discussion. How many times have I not argued with him, even when a young girl. He regarded no honest opinion as trivial and always found time for those who dissented from him — a quality rare in teachers in our country or in prophets anywhere. He was an untypical prophet also in that he did not lay claim to revelation. He held forth neither blandishment of reward nor fear of punishment. Nor was he weighed down by the burden of his mission. He was a saint who quipped and had use for laughter.

To me Gandhiji is a living man who represents the highest level to which a human being can evolve. Steeped in the best from the past he lived in the present, yet for the future. Hence the timelessness of his highest thoughts. Much that he said and wrote was for the solution of immediate problems. Some was for the inner guidance of individuals. His intellect did not feed on derived information. He fashioned his ideas as tools in the course of his experiments in the laboratory of his own life.

CHAPTER 4

The Anterooms of Power

You decided to live with your father at the residence of the Prime Minister, and to be the hostess, the housekeeper and the companion.

In 1950 the policy of non-alignment secured for India a world status far higher than that which her military strength and economic resources might otherwise entitle her. It meant continuous contacts with a wide cross section of nations and the leaders. You had the opportunity to observe the .finer points of summit diplomacy from the inside.

Throughout your father's seventeen year term as Prime Minister you were active at home in various capacities in your own right while not trusting yourself in the public eye. When you became a member of the Congress Working Committee you called it an "unexciting event".

In 1956 you became President of the Allahabad Congress Committee. That seemed quite natural. In 1957 you were elected to the Congress Central Election Committee. It was an interesting year as a Communist Government came to power in Kerala. This attracted a lot of attention abroad because it was the first time a Communist Government had come to power through constitutional means.

WHEN I WENT TO LIVE WITH MY FATHER AT TEEN MURTI House, the residence of the Prime Minister, it wasn't really a choice. My father asked me to come and to set up the house for him. There was nobody else to do it. So I set up the house, but I resisted every inch of the way about becoming a hostess. I was simply terrified of the so-called social duties. Although I met a large number of people, I wasn't good at "socializing" and small talk and that sort of thing. I had always hated parties. I said I would do everything behind the scenes but I was not going to appear before people.

I used to stay for a period of time and then go. Later, it became more and more difficult to leave. My husband was then working in Lucknow and I used to go there. But, invariably, I would get a telegram:

"Important guest coming return at once." My father would feel so hurt if I didn't come that it was very difficult to say no. It was a real problem because, naturally, Feroze didn't always appreciate my going away. I was living about half the month in Lucknow and half in Delhi, until Feroze became a member of the Constituent Assembly. Then, of course he came to Delhi and we could all be together. So I really grew into the work and life style. I had always thought that, once the house was set up, I could find a housekeeper. Now we have schools of catering and people are starting to work in hotels, but, at that time, we just didn't have anybody. An ordinary housekeeper wouldn't have done, because much of the work consisted of meeting people and taking that burden off my father, as well as looking after the guests. We always had guests staying at the house. We had guests at every meal, from breakfast to dinner.

For the women especially, it is a constant battle with protocol. It is like walking on a tight rope — to adhere close enough to the formal side of protocol so as not to offend even the most fastidious of dignitaries while managing not to stifle the human element and to keep the function interesting and homely. It is the daily struggle with menus to suit all tastes, the intricacies of decorating a State House, and so on.

Even such simple problems are made complicated in India by the peculiar fads of our people. Beside the main taboos of Hindus not eating beef and Muslims not eating pork, there are endless combinations and mutations. Some meateaters become vegetarians on certain days of the week; some vegetarians eat eggs, others eat fish as well, and one distinguished guest, who declared himself a vegetarian, ended up eating everything except chicken!

Even the quantity of food required can differ. I had an experience which could only occur in a nightmare, I thought. During our first year we had several receptions for diplomats and others at the in-between hour of 6.30 or 7 p.m. and I had discovered that very little food was consumed on these occasions. Then we gave a party for a slightly different crowd. On advice from the meteorological department we had planned it out of doors. Just as the guests were arriving, there was a sudden thunderstorm and we had to herd them indoors, where it was so hot that a couple of people fainted off. When the food was shown around, instead of helping themselves to just one *samosa* or sweet, some of the guests relieved the waiters of the entire dish! To our mounting dismay we saw the food exhausted even before all the guests had arrived. That sturdy standby — the *pakora* — saved the day, along with dried fruit and nuts! Strange as it may seem, neither my father nor his guests realized that anything was unusual. But since that dreadful day, I took good care to have extra food available, and to make duplicate arrangements for outside and inside, even if there wasn't a single cloud in the sky.

One year, during the Buddhist conference held on the occasion of the 2500th anniversary of Lord Buddha, we had arranged lunch for the delegates who included the Dalai Lama and many venerable monks. At the very last moment we realized that monks must have their last meal before noon while the other guests would not be free until 1.30. So we had 75 monks to lunch at 11.30 a.m. and 100 others at 1.30 p.m.

Almost every time my father went on a journey in India or abroad he would discover recipes or customs of which he approved and which we had to adopt. The first time he dined at Buckingham Palace he decided that in our house too the milk and sugar should be served before the coffee. This was often bewildering to our guests who looked around furtively to see if they had somehow mislaid, or forgotten to take, their coffee.

On another trip, he stayed at a country house and liked the idea of everybody helping themselves at breakfast. This suited us fine, for each one of us had his own activities and breakfast was a hurried meal. But again this was a habit which guests could not get used to and it ended with our having to serve them ourselves.

*　*　*

When it was first decided that we would move into the then Commander-in-Chief's residence, I went over to have a look at it and was at once plunged in gloom. Staring down from the walls of the public rooms were lifeless portraits of stern generals, resplendent in their bemedalled uniforms. I felt they were watching every movement, criticising every unspoken thought. I could not be at ease until they were all taken down and hurriedly despatched to the Defence Ministry. Their removal made the rooms look larger and the walls seemed to stretch in their stark bareness. Such enormous rooms, such long corridors! Could this ever be made livable, could it ever have any semblance of a home?

I need not have worried. Which house can resist fast-growing boys full of healthy noises and mischief, and a host of animals?

We had always had dogs, the good kind with long pedigrees, and others rescued off the streets which were just as devoted. We also had parrots, pigeons, squirrels and practically every small creature common in India. We thought life was pretty full, looking after them besides all, the other chores. Then, in Assam, we were presented with a baby cat-bear or red Himalayan Panda, although we did not know what it was until, we reached Agartala and were able to study the book of Indian animals in the Commissioner's library. The tribesmen had told us that it was a kind of bear expected to grow large and strong. The children decided to call it Bhimsa ("like Bhim") even before they had seen the tiny ball of fur. We arranged a corner for Bhimsa in the children's bathroom but somehow I could not house-train him and he always climbed on to the towel-rack to do his business, besides racing all over the house. Finally we banished him to the garden — a large wire-netting enclosure was built with a little wooden house in a tree. And that is where he has lived ever since — except when he went off to Nainital every summer. Much later we got him a wife, Pema (which means lotus in Sikkimese) and they had the most adorable little cubs — the first, I believe, to be born in captivity. My father used to call on the Panda family, morning and evening. They missed him when he was absent. Once, when he was ill, we even took Bhimsa to see him in his bedroom. The only things that made them unhappy were loud noises and the scent of dogs and tigers.

In 1955, we were offered our first tiger cubs — three of them named Bhim, Bhairav and Hidimba. A man came from the Lucknow

Zoo to look after them and advised us to have a cement floor in their enclosure. Unfortunately he put the cubs in before the cement had set properly, so that their paws were lacerated. Two were cured with sulphur powder but little Bhim got worse and worse. Without our knowledge the veterinary doctor on attendance decided to cauterize Bhim's paws, forgetting that despite his ferocious roar he was still a baby, he gave him such a large dose of sedative that he practically collapsed. My father and I were terribly upset. After much telephoning we were lucky to contact another vet, who prescribed saline injections and constant watching night and day. One of our reception officers opted to stay half the night while I would go to bed at 10 p.m. and get up at 2 a.m. to take my turn. On the fifth morning, Bhim raised his head. My children used to play with the cubs and did not care how boisterous they got, but for other children and visitors it was a boon to have Bhim still dazed and docile from his illness, and many who would not ordinarily come within ten yards of him felt courageous enough to stroke him. He recovered fast and soon was too big to be kept loose in a house with so much "va-et-viens." Reluctantly we sent them off to the Lucknow Zoo, where you can still meet Bhim and Hidimba, two magnificent beasts, their muscles rippling with power and grace. While they were at our house they were petted by many distinguished people including Marshal Tito and Prime Minister U. Nu. The Marshal asked for one of them and Bhairav now resides in Belgrade.

*   *   *

During the partition riots, I had saved several lives only to be rewarded by the worst abuse from both victims and attackers, each one being convinced that I had favoured the others. For months afterwards streams of refugees poured in. Everyday I sat solidly and patiently in one place between 8 a.m. and 1.30 p.m., and sometimes again in the afternoon, interviewing group after group.

My father would come too, but usually he would not stay. He would say a word or two and then I would find out what it was all about, what they wanted, what could be done. For the majority of them, there was not much one could do, except listen to their tales of woe. But apparently, even that gave them peace of mind. And there were always just enough cases within our power to help to keep up hope.

Along with this crowd came Satya, the 20-or-so-year-old daughter of a murdered railway level crossing keeper. As a child she had been run over and had lost both legs at the thighs. The only movement she could make was to drag herself on her hands. Consequently her body had become misshapen. It was a distressing sight. There was no way one could really help her except by providing artificial legs, and this I decided to do.

It was not an easy task. First, I discovered that the Artificial Limb Centre, in Poona, which catered exclusively for the armed forces, was the only institution in India capable of providing this service. Secondly, it took me months to persuade the then Defence Minister, Sardar Baldev Singh, to make an exception and to allow Satya to be admitted into the institution. This precedent, plus further efforts later, succeeded in opening the doors of the centre to civilians permanently. Several visits to Poona were required, as well as many painful months of patient endurance which were interspersed with fits of depression — dark moments when Satya felt it wasn't worthwhile to persevere and when she sought me out for reassurance. At last, her body was coaxed into normal shape and not only was she fitted with the final pair of legs but she learned to use them with the greatest self-assurance. She came to show off a little and to announce her engagement, her face transformed, glowing, positively scattering the gold dust of her happiness on all who happened to be near her.

Every now and then when I seem to be going around in circles, when my efforts seem so feeble compared with the immensity of the task, the memory of Satya's radiance, like Wordsworth and his daffodils, come to my mind and I cannot help smiling.

*   *   *

In 1950 the policy of non-alignment secured for India a world status far higher than that to which her military strength and economic resources might otherwise entitle her. It meant continuous contacts with a wide cross-section of nations and their leaders. I had the opportunity to observe the finest points of summit diplomacy from the inside. I went with my father on some of the trips. Before we

visited the United States, people like Sukarno, Hatta and others had
come and stayed with us. The Asian Relations Conference took place
before we moved to Teen Murti House and we were still in the small
York Road house. This is where many leaders from Asian countries
visited us.

The Chiang Kai Sheks were among them. My father was actually
their guest when the war broke out, and he returned there in
September 1939. So they visited us here. My father called me to
Delhi. Some of us women took Madame Chiang Kai Shek round the
city.

The Chiang Kai Sheks came at a time when I was extremely busy
as I was going to get married. I was a bit self-centered in a way at that
moment, but it seemed to me that Madam Chiang Kai Shek was a
person who was very charming, very elegant, rather removed from the
realities of life. Unlike my parents who were so close to the people, the
poor people, they were rich, belonging to the upper class, to the aristocracy. In a country like China how could it last?

In 1949 we went to the United States. I had gone in a private capacity. I may have gone to one banquet but I didn't attend anything
else. I went with my father in President Truman's plane. Mrs. Pandit
was our ambassador in the United States and she advised my father
that I shouldn't come officially. I wonder whether she thought it
would affect her position. I remember that Homi Bhaba[1] happened to
be in Washington and used to take me out to meals, as otherwise I
would have been all alone. I had known Homi from long before
Independence and he was a good friend, so interested and interesting.
The Trumans were very nice people; a very affectionate couple.

Then we went to Indonesia. Sukarno was one of the most colourful
persons. We met him more in the earlier days before his life took on a
different turn. In these days we noticed his passionate devotion to
Indonesia, the sort of thing we felt for India. This was the greatest
bond. We liked him as a person. But the greatest bond was that he
had the same sort of feeling: he was not just for freedom, for a national government, but he wanted to improve every individual there. He
used to stop his car in the street and ask a man: can you sing the

---

1. Atomic scientist and founder of the Trombay Atomic Energy Centre. He was
   killed in a plane crash a few years later.

national anthem? and they both stood and sang the national anthem. He was in a way a teacher of the country as my father was here. Like my father, he was giving long speeches. He was really educating the people.

Many people used to criticise my father and ask why he gave such long speeches. He was really educating the people and he used to talk even to the village people about science: how science was changing life, changing attitudes of mind and affecting the world in a way that the world hadn't experienced for all the thousands of years previously.

On our journey to Indonesia we also went to Singapore and probably Penang.

In 1953 we went to China. I met Chou En-Lai and Mao Tse-Tung. Mao didn't come to India. I was told later that he was waiting for an invitation. If only we had called him, many things would have been different. Had we known it then, he would have been most welcomed and honoured by this country.

I liked Chou En-Lai. He was very well informed. Of the people we met in China, he was the only one who had been abroad. He was much more sophisticated and *au courant* with foreign affairs. He saw things in a little different perspective.

Then we attended the Coronation ceremony in London. We had an Indian Ambassadors' meeting in Switzerland. We stayed in Burgenstock where Charlie Chaplin came to meet us, and from there I went to the Soviet Union for a rest with our Ambassador, Mr. K.P.S. Menon, and his wife. We heard the news that foreigners would be allowed to travel in the USSR at the Prague Airport while we were refuelling. So we spent the whole month travelling all over the Soviet Union.

I didn't have anything to do with any Soviet officials but they put a plane at our disposal. Our party consisted of Mr. and Mrs. Menon, Mr. Prakash Kaul, who was then First Secretary in the Embassy, and myself.

We were accompanied by a man from the Soviet Protocol, another from the Tourist Department and an interpreter called Maya. I enjoyed that visit. It was quite non-political. We saw a great deal and the people were very welcoming.

In 1955, I returned to the Soviet Union — officially and with my father this time. We had a tremendous welcome. Of course, in China we had had a very warm welcome from the people, and I believe the

Soviet leaders looked at the film of that trip and thought that they shouldn't do less than the Chinese.

Then, our people saw films of our welcome in the USSR. That is why Bulganin and Khrushchev had such a tumultuous welcome in India. I was chairman of the Committee which made all the arrangements for the visit. While they were in India, the changing roles of the two, with Khrushchev coming on top became apparent. When they arrived, they were equal but, by the time they left, Khrushchev was already walking ahead. In lots of small ways you could see that Khrushchev was putting Bulganin in this place and that the latter didn't answer back. In the beginning, you couldn't take them through a small door because they had to walk side by side.

We had a small cultural show for them in a tiny open-air theatre and I thought that since the Vice-President and my father were accompanying them, one could go with the Vice-President and one could go with my father. The Russian leaders said that it simply couldn't be done. They insisted that the two cars should go abreast, which wasn't possible because of the narrowness of the road.

They were thrilled with their visit because it was the first time either of them had been out of the Soviet Union and had had such a spontaneous and friendly welcome. In their country, of course, they usually travelled in closed cars.

*   *   *

My father was Prime Minister for seventeen years. Meanwhile, I was active at home in various capacities. From 1955, I devoted less time to welfare work and more to politics; I continued with child welfare though. I was President of the Indian Council for Child Welfare and Vice-President of the International Union of Child Welfare. I also started a children's cooperative in Delhi known today as the Bal Sahayog.[1]

I was on the Social Welfare Board when it was started. Actually I was in Moscow when I got a telegram about it; so it may have been

---

1. In a one storey building near Connaught Place in Delhi the boys do carpentry, tailoring, woodwork and canework. Some dig in the garden and grow plants in the fairly spacious grounds around.

formed as early as 1953. Sometime in between, I had criticised the functioning of the Congress and the Congress President answered: "You have no business criticising from outside, if you want to, you'd better see how it works and do something about it." Then he put me in charge of organizing the women's department. We didn't have a separate women's wing until then. I think I was in charge of both, women and youth. I don't know the precise date but I remember that I had the flu when the President of the Congress telephoned that he wanted to see me. I said I was very sorry but I had a terrible fever and I couldn't get up.

Then they would come to my bedroom, he announced. Finally a compromise was reached and I came in my dressing gown to meet them in the room next to my bedroom, a small dining room which we used in the winter because it was warmer. The President of the Congress and Mr. Lal Bahadur came to tell me that they wanted to nominate me to the Working Committee.

Long before all this, in 1951, I had started accompanying my father on his election tours. When we went to Himachal Pradesh — and that was one of the first places we went to — the Himachal people had asked me to be their representative in Parliament in 1952. I answered that I didn't want to stand as a candidate. But they insisted that they wanted to have a woman and asked me to suggest a name. I mentioned Rajkumari Amrit Kaur's name and promised that I would go on the election tour in Himachal Pradesh. This is how I came to accompany my father.

Previously, when Gandhiji was still alive, Mr. Pant[1] had asked me to come to Uttar Pradesh politics or at least to join the Assembly. I said no categorically. He complained to Gandhiji and said:

Look at this slip of a girl who thinks she is much cleverer than I am.

When I said I didn't think I was capable of assuming such functions, Pantji answered:

Would I make such a proposal if I had not assessed the situation and assessed her capabilities?

---

1. Govind Vallabh Pant, Congress leader from Uttar Pradesh who later became Home Minister in the Nehru Government.

I did not volunteer to go. I was horrified at the idea. Gandhiji asked what I had done to Pantji who was so angry; had I been rude to him? I said I was never rude to anybody. I repeated what I said and added that this was my honest opinion. I didn't think that I was cut out for that type of work. Besides, just then, my children were too small. Gandhiji laughed and agreed that I shouldn't take it too seriously, but that Pantji was very upset, and he thought he had better let me know.

*   *   *

During one of my father's campaigns, the people from a place called Chamba had written to him saying that they would like him to go there and my father had accepted their invitation. When we arrived at Pathankot, Rajkumari was there to meet us. She said she couldn't fit Chamba into the programme and she had arranged for my father to speak only in her constituency — which was pretty large. The Chamba people were so upset that they even wept. They said: "Now we have lost, because we have no credibility." We said we would come anyway and they said: "You will never come to an out-of-the-way place like Chamba."

My father didn't know what to do because his schedule was so tight that he couldn't possibly add to it. So we sat in the car (I was in the front between the driver and security guard) and we asked ourselves what we could do for the people of Chamba. I was feeling rather bad because I knew my father had agreed to go there. I asked the driver how many miles it was to Chamba and how long it would take. This was on the last days of the campaign. In order to give a speech, we had to reach there before midnight the next day.

We reached Mandi at 2 O'clock in the morning. There I confessed to my father, while going to bed, that I was so upset about the Chamba people that the thought had come to my mind that perhaps I could go and say that you had accepted their invitation, but for unavoidable reasons it was not possible for you to come and that I was bringing your greetings. I added that the driver had said that there was no way at all I could be there on time and that, of course, I didn't know whether I would be able to do it, because I hadn't done any electioneering recently. But at least that much I could say. I thought he would say: "Nonsense, you shouldn't go."

But he immediately replied that one way I could go was to fly to Pathankot as Chamba was only 150 or so miles from there.

He said that it was very late any way and that we had to leave before 6.00 in the morning. When I got up in the morning, there was a slip of paper under my door saying: "You will be dropped at Pathankot!"

In Chamba they had arranged for me to stay in the Circuit House. I said that, since I was there as a representative of my father's party, I didn't think it was proper for me to stay in the Circuit House. There seemed nowhere else to go to.

"What about the candidate?"

They said I couldn't stay with them.

"Why not? Hasn't he got a wife or a daughter or any woman in the house?"

Yes, he had a wife and a daughter but I couldn't possibly stay there, they said.

"Why not?" I answered, "I can stay where they stay, I am used to all kinds of places."

*   *   *

I was so determined that I won the argument. So two stories went round. One, that I couldn't be Panditji's daughter, because I would never stop in these sort of places. The other, that I must be Panditji's daughter because no one else would have given up the comfort and good service of the Circuit House, to go and stay in a tiny house. That meeting was a great success and from then on there was such a demand for me to go to places where my father couldn't go that I couldn't accompany him any more and had to go electioneering on my own.

I also became deeply involved in my husband's election, because, as he pointed out, we had such a short time and his constituency was so large that he couldn't possibly cover it all by himself. He just drew a line and said:

This half is yours and this half is mine.

By then, I wasn't worried any longer about my father's constituency. Rae Bareli, my husband's constituency is so placed that it stands between Allahabad and Lucknow.

*   *   *

So, when my tour ended on one side I would spend the night in Anand Bhavan in Allahabad, and when it ended on the other side I would sleep in Lucknow where my husband was based. The children also were there, but my father's home was in Allahabad. Usually the places I had to visit were too far from Rae Bareli itself which was my husband's headquarters and he was covering the area around there.

On one of the Allahabad visits I found that nobody had done anything about appointing polling agents for my father. By that time, I had got bronchitis and I remember having a high temperature. I had to sign many papers. Then, there were hundreds of people visiting. They came to Anand Bhavan as winter was the time of the big fair. They would shout for me to come out. I did not know what to do: either get the signing done or go to meet the people. The doctor said I had to stay in bed, I couldn't be up with bronchitis, and she was giving me injections every four hours. Finally, I solved the problem by sitting at the dining table and signing the papers and allowing people to pass through and look at me at the same time. We had a constant stream of people from all parts of the country passing by and sometimes shouting slogans or saying something while I was signing these hundreds of forms and settling who would be the polling agents.

In 1956 I became President of the Allahabad Congress Committee. The only thing that bothered me about this nomination was that Allahabad had always had a lot of quarrels; the local politicians had even tried to get my mother mixed up in group politics. I was very much aware of it then. When she was arrested, my mother feared that groupism might worsen in her absence. So she had instructed me to go and meet some people and to tell them certain things. Now I remember all that but, fortunately, while I was City President, I managed to keep quarrels in abeyance. I can't say that they disappeared but they did not erupt.

*   *   *

In 1957 I was elected to the Congress Central Election Committee. I had not been a candidate, I didn't want to stand, but Mr. U.N. Dhebar[1] informed me that they had sent up my name and that I could not refuse. As it happened, all but four people voted for me. Had I won by say 80% or less, nobody would have bothered to wonder who had voted for me, but since there were only four dissenters, I was terribly concerned to know who they were and this bothered me for a long time. Eventually, I found out the name of one of them.

I also remember that there was a tie between two South Indians. One was Mr. Mallaya and the other Mr. Nijalingappa[2]. I didn't know very well, so I went to my father to ask him whom one should vote for. But my father never helped me in such matters; he just replied: "You are now on your own." Then I went to the other leaders and learned what a poor opinion they had of Mr. Nijalingappa!

For the general elections of 1957, I campaigned all over the country. Mr. Shastri, who was then Railway Minister, was put in charge of the elections and this is really why he resigned. There was a railway accident and everybody thought that he had resigned his ministership merely because of the accident. It may have had something to do with it, but one reason was the elections.

Mr. Shastri used to take a lot of work off my father's shoulders; I worked very closely with him concerning the candidates and he would phone me wherever I was, because every day I was sent to a different place. In fact, this was the year before the elections, when Rajiv had to have an operation and I spent the day and night in the hospital with him. That was just the time when Shastriji wanted to call people from Uttar Pradesh to discuss the list of candidates for that State. I pleaded: "Please, I simply can't do it on that particular day." He insisted that the dates had been fixed; I was sorry but the date of the operation had also been fixed for over a month and I couldn't change it. The doctor too was very busy and my son had to go back to school after the operation. At first, Shastriji was horrified that the child should be operated on. He was very much against operations and he asked if I had tried any other medicines and methods. I asked him to handle the

---

1. Dhebar was the President of the Congress.
2. Nijalingappa, a political leader from Mysore State who became President of the Congress. It is under his presidentship that the split of the Party occurred.

question of the election list himself and afterwards, if necessary, I could meet the people. But suddenly I found them all trooping into the hospital, so we had the meeting there. They put chairs outside on the verandah.

*   *   *

That year a Communist government came to power in Kerala. This attracted a lot of attention abroad because for the first time this had happened through constitutional means. But I want to say something about Kerala because the Marxists are always accusing me of having brought down their government. My recollection is that Mr. Namboodripad, who was the Chief Minister, did make a statement to the effect that the law and order situation was not entirely in their control, there was a strong public demand for a change of government. But it could never have been done had the Central Government not been willing. I did go to Kerala and I did report on the situation. My own opinion would not have changed things. The fact is that my father probably was not happy about the situation. I know Feroze was not happy about it. But I also know that people like Mr. Pant, the then Home Minister, and others were determined that it should happen. So my part was not as important as it is now made out to have been.

I never argued with the President of India, Dr. Rajendra Prasad, at any stage. I either went to the limit of my contacts among important people, such as Mr. Dhebar, my predecessor, or Mr. Shastri or Mr. Govind Vallabh Pant. I didn't talk to anybody else. Later on, Mr. T.T. Krishnamachari used to come frequently to see my father and as he often had to wait, I got to know him well and then I talked freely with him. But I never had a discussion with the President so far as I can remember.

I may have just gone and reported to him but I would never argue with him.

*   *   *

Regarding Maharashtra and Gujarat, my view was that we couldn't avoid linguistic separation. So the choice was very limited. I was positive we would lose the election in Gujarat and Maharashtra and, on both sides, parties would come in who were committed to separation. Then once the Assembly would have voted for separation, what would we have gained?

My opinion was formed in response to the feelings of the people and as an assessment that division couldn't be avoided. If you can't avoid something you should handle it in the best way possible. It was not a question of principle because we had agreed to linguistic States everywhere else. But this decision was taken long before Independence. One of the plans of the Congress programme was linguistic States. This drew people towards the Congress because people felt highly emotional about such matters.

When, much later, the question of the separation within Andhra Pradesh arose, there again it was not a matter of principle. I saw no reason why a State which had the same language should separate and I stuck to my decision, even though everybody, including the President of India, thought I would have to give in.

CHAPTER 5

The Leader of the Congress Party

In February 1959, at Nagpur, you were elected President of the Indian National Congress.

Before Independence three women held the office of President of the Indian National Congress, but since Independence you have been the only woman to be the head of the Congress Party. You thus gave your family the distinction of providing India with a three generation line of Congress Presidents. Your grandfather, Motilal Nehru, was President for two terms in 1919 and 1928 and your father, Jawaharlal Nehru, held the office for six one-year terms, four of them during the Prime Ministership.

This was the first event of this magnitude in your political life.

During your tenure as President of the Congress a great amount of clarity came to the Party but you were not really able to alter significantly its structure, the old set-up and the way it used to approach problems and to function.

On 15 August 1959, in your Independence Day message, you said: "In mountaineering, the higher one climbs, the more hazardous the journey and the narrower and steeper the trail." It seems that the Congress Party then refused to climb the slope with you, because to climb the slope needed the same calibre or at least the same vision of the world. One has the impression that, at that time, you were far ahead.

In 1960 a personal tragedy occurred: your husband, Feroze Gandhi, passed away.

In 1960 you resumed your political activities and you were very active in all the Congress bodies. In 1962 the General Election took place. You campaigned for the Party. You had become a popular figure of all India standing.

In October 1962, the Chinese attacked. You were a member of the Government's National Defence Council and the Chairman of the Central Citizen's Council and you showed a militant nationalism and an extraordinary courage.

On 21 November 1962 there was a unilateral cease-fire.

On 18 April 1964, on your way to the World Fair in New York, you stated: "I do not want to be in the Government." That is why one had then the feeling that, while one part of your personality was tempted by political leadership, the other was craving for a greater intimacy, peace and security of private life.

On 27 May 1964, Mr. Nehru passed away. He had been Prime Minister for 17 years. Many people in India and abroad thought that the Indian political system would not survive and predicted all sorts of disasters. Of course, the passing of Nehru's charismatic leadership left its mark on Indian politics. It was the end of an epoch.

When Mr. Shastri became Prime Minister you accepted the portfolio of the Ministry of Information and Broadcasting.

In 1965 war broke out between India and Pakistan. You played a magnificent role in maintaining Indian morale and you were described at that time as "the only man in a Cabinet of old women."

On 10 January 1966, after signing the Tashkent agreement which put an end to a 22 days' war with Pakistan, Mr. Shastri, "the well-meaning and honest man" who had succeeded your father hardly nineteen months before, passed away.

IN FEBRUARY 1959, I WAS ELECTED PRESIDENT OF THE INDIAN National Congress at the Nagpur Session. This was a most important event in my political life. A few questions were asked at that time by political observers: had my father deliberately groomed me as his political heir? Or was he averse to the idea? Did he compromise my independence of thought or action? Could I remain in the public eye without attracting adverse comment? Was I able to stand for myself in Indian politics without compromising my independence as a woman? Finally, would my role have been easier if

I had been my father's son rather than his daughter? These questions are not really for me to answer. All I can say is how I tried to fulfil what I considered to be my task.

I used to go to the office absolutely on the dot, at nine in the morning. At 2.30 I would return home unless there was a lunch party that my father wanted me to be present at, in which case I would come home a few minutes earlier.

We innovated in that, for the first time, the Congress office was open to all, and we had more than 50 Members of Parliament helping us in the evening and over the week-end.

Refugees were still coming in. We had a Grievance Office to deal with the problems of Muslims and other questions like land and so on. Previously, there had been a Foreign Department but no specific office to deal with minorities. We also had somebody to deal with the press and a lot of journalists would come and sit around as the office became a centre for various activities.

I also travelled extensively. Not only to every State except Orissa, but to almost every district in every State. And yet, at the time, I was suffering from the most excruciating pain because I had a stone in my kidney. The pain continued for almost a year. It was discovered either immediately after my election or a day or two before.

While I was Congress President, I organized a seminar to discuss the next plan. It was Mr. Dhebar's idea originally, but I followed it up. We called on all the parties to attend this seminar. Ashok Mehta, then the chairman of the Praja Socialist Party, and various other people came and we spent a week together having discussions. Incidentally, this is when I read the novel *Lolita*, which had been sent to my father for him to see whether it should be banned or not.

Generally speaking, I would say the Party became much more action-oriented in those days. Another thing I initiated was the training of cadres.

In Gandhigram we trained 100 people and I collected money for that purpose. I put aside Rs. 100,000 for the employment of these people. However, the President who succeeded me didn't think it was important enough. As a result not only did these people lose their jobs, but the money was directed for other purposes.

When I was elected, the Congress was in debt. I put its finances right and left money in all the departments.

One area in which I could not manage to bring about significant alterations was the structure of the Congress Party. That was a question of high policy and I couldn't do anything. All the big-wigs were always in the Working Committee. Therefore, it was impossible to bring in anybody new. You couldn't have a special guest or introduce some very young person. So I persuaded my father and some others to leave the formal membership of the Working Committee and young people were taken in as permanent invitees. For the regular membership, we arranged an entirely new set-up, a much younger one. I wouldn't call it a change of structure but rather a change of outlook — for the first time, some new people came in and some of the State political leaders such as Atulya Ghosh, who had become immovable, were changed, although they continued to attend and advise.

Then I undertook *padyatras*. Lots of other people did walk. The idea was that everyone should go and walk in his constituency and get to know the people. Although, I must admit that mine were not very fair *padyatras* in the real sense of the word. The local Congress accepted so many engagements that I couldn't possibly cover so many miles on foot. The Opposition tried to make much of this. But the people replied that I myself had called it a "jeepyatra." The person who had organized my schedule at that time allowed me hardly ten minutes at one place and then, some miles further another ten minutes. So it was just impossible. We walked within the villages but we couldn't do more.

*   *   *

In my Independence Day message, on 15 August 1959, I said: "In mountaineering, the higher one climbs the more hazardous the journey and the narrower and steeper the trail." Unfortunately, then the Congress Party seemed to refuse to climb the slope with me. People generally like to take the easier road. Even to Badrinath there are now buses. And after all, it is faith — whatever the kind — which drives a person on. Either a religious creed or faith in an ideology. It can be to the right or to the left. But most people prefer the middle of the road. They lack that kind of drive. So, it is difficult to get people moving. For instance, take the Emergency. When it was decided, most of our Members of Parliament were quite upset. They couldn't understand the situation. Then they went to their constituencies and, when they realized that the people had welcomed the decision, their attitude changed because they are dependent on their people. When the people say it is a good thing, they cannot say otherwise. But they should decide for themselves whether something is good or not. I mean the people may say it is a good thing when it is the opposite. In fact most people were saying that the Emergency should have been proclaimed long ago. And I agree with them. Had we taken some action earlier, it need not have been so drastic. It could have been a lesser action which at that time, would have been more effective. But, because we waited so long, it was not possible to take the lesser course of action.

The Nagpur session of the Congress in 1959 was also an important one as it adopted the controversial resolution on cooperative farming which laid down joint cooperative farming as the future model for Indian agriculture. But to implement this resolution the Party had to break with its old methods. And I proved unable to alter the Party's structure or approach significantly on this problem. They kept saying that implementation of the Nagpur resolution meant that the land would be taken away from the peasants. Widespread propaganda was launched to the effect that it was not cooperative farming but collective farming. This created such a reaction in Parliament and outside that it became impossible to proceed with it.

This big conflict has always existed since the Congress is a party of many opinions. Its members vote for various resolutions because they are popular. But a large number of M.P.s don't have faith in them. The so-called bosses of the Party were the ones more to the right; they took most of their ideas from the West. That is why the Nagpur Resolution could not be implemented. Nor any other land reform. We kept on passing resolutions but it seemed impossible to implement them.

* * *

In addition to dealing with internal matters, I also emphasised international affairs: Congress solidarity with anti-colonial movements, establishment of a National Committee for Africa, creation of the Indian Council for Africa, condemnation of racialism

With Feroze Gandhi on board the ship on her return from England in 1941

At home with her father and her sons

Indira, when she became President of the Congress in 1959, in the garden of her ancestral
home at Anand Bhawan (above) and at the 1959 Nagpur Session of the All India Congress
Committee (below)

With Presidents Tito and Nasser at the 1960 Tripartite meeting in Delhi

Indira with President Bhutto

At Paris with President De Gaulle, Madame De Gaulle, Prime Minister
Georges Pompidou and Madame Pompidou in 1966

As a member of the executive council of UNESCO (1962)

At Washington with President and Jacqueline Kennedy in 1961

in South Africa and British Nyasaland. In fact, I had a long-standing sympathy for any nationalism or any fight against colonial rule. Since my visit to South Africa this was reinforced because of what I saw there. Of course, I also had great sympathy for the Algerian struggle, largely because of the stories we heard of the great courage of the Algerian women.

Most of the African leaders are old personal friends. I had met them before. Both President Nyerere of Tanzania and President Kaunda of Zambia came to India. One year Kaunda, the next year Nyerere. They are both very sincere and dedicated people. Kaunda has a bond with Gandhiji's thought and teachings which is emotional whereas Nyerere is much more intellectual and has a very acute understanding of the forces which are moving, especially in the developing world. It is always very stimulating to talk to him.

I was also impressed by President Nyerere of Tanzania. He is a man of vision and balance. He is actually an example in Africa. He has clear ideas and knows how to handle his people and situations. People tend to get either excited or blown off by influences and pressures, but he has held on firmly to what he considered to be the good of Tanzania.

I toured some African countries in 1960. I couldn't go to Zambia which was then Northern Rhodesia. But Mr. Kaunda sent Mr. Kapapwe, the Minister with whom he has since fallen out. He sent him to me to ask me to go to their country, but my programme was fixed and I couldn't make it.

*   *   *

Then, in 1960, I lost my husband. Within a year I resumed all my political activities. I felt I had to be occupied. I went to Mexico just a few months after Feroze died. I had put off that visit twice and the Mexicans were getting quite annoyed about it. The Ministry of External Affairs felt it would not be good to postpone it again. From Mexico I went to the United States where I gave the Howland Memorial Lecture in Yale University. I have always been fascinated by Mexico, by Latin America in general and by both the Maya and the Inca civilisations. I think Mexico is an extraordinary country. That year when I was nominated to the Unesco Executive Board, Dr. Radhakrishnan[1] felt I should have more work.

* * *

In 1962 we had a General Election. I campaigned for the Party. I was then Chairman of the Congress National Integration Council. This was the time of the Jabalpur riots and we had to attack communalism and to speak up in favour of minority rights. Mahatma Gandhi and my father had always recognised communalism as one of the biggest dangers to India's very survival. The communal spirit was responsible for the partition of India in 1947 and, before that, for the weakening of the national movement. For instance, in the 1930s one of our prom .ent leaders, Ganeshan Jathi, was killed in such a communal riot, when he had gone only to bring peace.

Communal harmony and the policy of what we call secularism is not against any religion; it respects all religions and stands for the equality for all citizens of India, regardless of their religion or their caste.

We give great importance to this policy because we think it is one of the cementing factors of India's unity. Without unity, of course, there can be no stability or progress. A person is less than human when he deprives somebody of his citizens' rights only because of his religion. There is something very wrong indeed with a person who thinks that way. And I feel the same way about racialism or any discrimination based on race, colour or sex for that matter.

* * *

In October 1962, the Chinese attacked, because of the Tibet situation. I felt it was very unfortunate because if all the countries of Asia could be more united, it would be much easier to solve the problems of this continent. India certainly doesn't want to be a leader but we do want to be strong enough to be able to defend ourselves and to solve our own problems. On the other hand, the Chinese have very strong views about their own superiority as a people and as a

---

Then President of India. Formerly Member of the Executive Board of Unesco.

nation. What the basis was for their attack, I do not know. I think the effects of it will show up only much later.

We had border problems and this is a question about which people get very excited. There are moments when one should try to be cool and say, well, just let it lie for a while. I am sure if they had taken that attitude, we could have solved the problem later on. But they chose the aggressive way. Maybe, they thought that they would frighten us. It was unfortunate and it certainly increased our burden very much. But, as a member of the Government's National Defence Council, I could not let them intimidate us. I viewed the Tibetan problem as a human one. There were people who were being oppressed and who asked for shelter. I was not questioning China's sovereignty or anything like that, but I did feel that, when people were coming to seek refuge, it had always been India's tradition to grant it.

I was opposed to the Chinese bringing their troops there. But I think we had accepted the view that Tibet had a very close relationship with China. I first met the Dalai Lama and the Panchen Lama in Peking when I was there with my father. I was impressed by the Dalai Lama. Later they came to India. Now the Dalai Lama lives up in Dharamsala.

On the 21st of November 1962, there was a unilateral cease fire. As a result of the war, Krishna Menon, the Defence Minister, left the Government. This departure was a loss to the Government. He had his fads but he was very lucid and a great patriot. He saw the problems very clearly and he had extraordinary ability for finding solutions. The reason for his leaving was not simply that people didn't like him. It was part of it, but the main reason was that they thought his departure would weaken my father. That was their aim. We saw a repetition of this tactic much later when they tried to attack everybody they thought was close to me. Although my father did regard Krishna Menon as a friend, I wouldn't say that he was as close to him as people made him out to be. I am sure he took his advice on many matters but he made up his mind on his own, and not because Krishna had said so.

I was a member of the National Defence Council, not in a personal capacity, but as Chairman of the Central Citizens' Council, the creation of which was entirely my idea. It became really effective after the war was over. It helped resettling the people of the affected areas around, and the handicapped.

I myself went to Tezpur in the North-East Frontier Agency (NEFA) where the withdrawal of the Indian Army caused panic. I am surprised now that I did not think of going there earlier. Mr. Bhagwati, who is now the head of the Indian National Trade Union Congress (INTUC), came to see me one day. He was so worried and looked so anxious that I didn't even listen to what he said. I just asked whether he thought that I should go. This he welcomed enthusiastically. Just then, father happened to be passing by. I rushed out, and informed him that I wanted to go to Tezpur. He said that he was on his way to a Cabinet meeting and that he would consult some of his colleagues. I knew they would never agree. He went and, sure enough, everybody said that it was not the right thing to do, that it would be very difficult. How could I go as there was no regular service, etc. I got hold of the Cabinet Secretary, Mr. S. S. Khera, who had come to see my father. I asked him to get me, by hook or by crook, on any plane going to Tezpur. I was ready to leave any time because I didn't need any luggage. Fortunately, he agreed that it was a good idea, and I was put on a plane at 4.00 the next morning.

I didn't think it was an act of courage, because I never felt that was doing something dangerous. It was a mere reflex. Something happens to you and you react in a particular way. Actually, Mr. Shastri also went; but not to Tezpur. He went to Gauhati and he tried keep me there too. He was with the Assam Cabinet and I had to wait. I waited an hour and a half and I was getting pretty fed up because it was getting dark. I knew that if it got dark they would say that I could not go. Shastriji said that the Assam Chief Minister was very upset. So I didn't say anything about going to Tezpur at all. I simply said I was going out, and I went. I got on to an army plane and flew to Tezpur. As I was waiting for a plane to be ready I could see that lots of people were panicking, even in Gauhati. Lots of women came and grabbed my legs, asking me to take them with me. They thought that I was going to Delhi.

The Army was also against my going to Tezpur. In fact, the Army is always opposed to anyone going to a military area.

Once I got there, I was able to encourage the local people, specially young people. I also went around the various places where the soldiers were, and wherever I went, they were glad. The conditions were rather bad. The camps were set up hastily as there was heavy rain.

The Citizens Council really did a good job. It was composed mostly of women. In all the States, either the Governor's wife or the Chief Minister's wife headed the Council. One of the most efficient of our members was the wife of the Punjab Chief Minister, Mrs. Kairon. I remember one incident. We had to send jeeps to fetch prisoners of war. They phoned at about 7.00 p.m. on a Saturday evening, saying that the Chinese insisted that whoever went should be dressed in white from head to foot. It was bitterly cold and all the uniforms were khaki. We had nothing white at all. We didn't have sheets that our people could have torn. They had to leave the next day by 11.00 a.m. or so. I didn't know how many white covers they needed but it was quite a large number, because, not only the drivers, but all those who went, like doctors and so on, had to be in white. First, I phoned everybody I knew in Delhi. All the shops were closed. All the tailors were off work. It may have been Sunday evening, I don't remember very precisely. Every woman I tried to get hold of was out. Finally we reached a few. They managed to get through back doors and get some shops open to collect white material. We didn't even have money at that moment, but we promised to pay for the material later. The women sat up all night and we had a pile of overalls ready by 4.00 in the morning. I went to the airport to put them on the plane and by 12.00 we had a call from the frontier, saying that the clothes had arrived and the party all dressed in white had just left.

*   *   *

When the war was over, we had re-settlement requests. I had gone to the frontier area and one of my party was hit by a bullet. Lots of stray bullets were lying around. We were just walking along and it went up his trouser leg. It was a surface wound only.

Once we received a request for sheep. We were told that wherever the Chinese had been, they had brainwashed the people somewhat, and that something needed to be done to resettle them. We were asked whether we could send some sheep because it would help those people to keep occupied on farms. Until then, nobody had paid any attention to these very remote areas. Once again, I called all the neighbouring areas asking whether anybody could let us have a few sheep. I thought it would take some time. But within five or six days, I got a call back saying that some hundreds of sheep were on their way to Delhi.

"But I have nowhere to put them, why didn't you let me know before; can't you delay by a day?"

The person on the telephone answered: "We have now told every village that they must give two or three or as many sheep as they can and we are paying for them. They are to bring them to the main road and we will send trucks to pick them up. Now, we simply cannot send another message to all these people. Some of them are coming from remote areas, and many trucks are arriving."

Then I went to the President and begged: "Can I have a garage or something? Can you leave your cars out in the open for one night, because it will take me at least that long to find another place, and a train to send them over?"

*   *   *

After the war, my father's health deteriorated; he probably wasn't well before, but Krishna Menon's departure was a very big blow to him. I think what hurt him most was that his own colleagues had been so opposed to him and the manner in which they had literally hounded Krishna Menon out of the Cabinet. If my father could have withstood that it would have been better, but the movement was so big and all the people he considered very close, T.T. Krishnamachari, Shastriji and all, were against him. It was a great disappointment.

All this weakened his position considerably and in that sense, one can say that the Government moved to the right at that point because none of the programmes were implemented. Of course, the "Syndicate"[1] had always existed but it had never been so visible or so compact. It really emerged at that time.

---

1. It was a team of State Congress leaders including Kamaraj, Atulya Ghosh, Sanjiva Reddy, Nijalingappa and S.K. Patil.

This was the time of the so-called Kamaraj Plan under which leading Cabinet Ministers and six provincial Chief Ministers were asked to resign their governmental offices in order to apply themselves to organisational work for the Congress Party.[1]

It seems that Mr. Kamaraj, Mr. Sanjiva Reddy and others got together at Tirupati and talked about it. Mr. Biju Patnaik just happened to be there. He overheard all of this, dashed back North and presented it as his plan. I was in Pahalgam with my father. As my father was resting after lunch, I went to the garden and sat with Mr. Patnaik who put this proposal to me. Naturally I didn't know that it was Mr. Kamaraj's idea. I asked:

"Well, how will they take it?"

"I can convince them," he replied.

Then my father came down and I left them together. Much later we heard it was really Mr. Kamaraj's plan.

I am told that Mr. Patnaik did the same sort of thing at the time of my election.

* * *

In 1964 the Congress met at Bhubaneswar and an important resolution was passed on democracy and socialism. These are actually two important concepts with so many interpretations and applications. I don't remember the exact words of the resolution. I think it was similar to what we are saying today, that a country of India's size and diversity can only be kept together by some form of democratic government, that is, a regime where the people's voice is heard and where the people can participate and feel involved in the development of their own region as well as in that of the country, and in all policies. And socialism is also imperative in a country which has so much poverty — although in terms of mere figures, as otherwise, I don't think our poverty is greater than that of other developing countries. The poor show up more in India because we also have the

---

1. Among these were Morarji Desai, Jagjivan Ram, Lal Bahadur Shastri, S.K. Patil, Kamaraj Nadar himself and . . . all contenders for the succession. Kamaraj Nadar who was Chief Minister of Madras, himself resigned to take up the Congress Presidentship, a post which he would occupy for the next four years.

very rich. African countries have great poverty also but their populations are much smaller and more scattered, and so less visible. In the circumstances of India, equality is imperative, not only for the human reason of not allowing people to suffer, but even to make democracy work. Democracy implies equality and therefore it implies socialism. Some people talk of nationalisation and of the State as the only entrepreneur. That is another concept of socialism which is not ours. Our socialism comprises a mixed economy, but gives greater importance to the State sector. Whether it works or not is another matter. But, even if we had the other kind, a purely State-controlled economy, I don't know that it would have worked better. In other countries, there was a big time lag before things started moving.

In fact, the Bhubaneswar resolution was not really very new. None of our resolutions are, because they are all based on thinking that has gone on over the years. Whether we do anything or not now, all these matters were thought of in their outline or in a broad perspective. Every resolution has pinpointed something and tried to bring clarity or greater emphasis on some aspect.

In fact, until I was in the Working Committee I never knew what the Working Committee did except what I read in the papers. I was quite close to Mr. Shastri, largely because of his own attitude. But my father never spoke to me about Government matters. Never. I mean I didn't ask him, and he never volunteered any information on what the Government was doing. He never said anything, but his colleagues did. I mean, Mr. Shastri would tell me and also Mr. T.T. Krishnamachari.

* * *

My father died on the 27th of May. He had been Prime Minister for seventeen years. Many people in India and abroad thought that the Indian political system would not survive and predicted all sorts of disasters.

Then Mr. Shastri became Prime Minister. I remember that, sometime before my father's death, an American called Welles Hangen[1] had asked who would succeed him. Without hesitation I had

---

1. Welles Hangen, author of the book *After Nehru Who?* Hart-Davis, London, 1963.

said: Mr. Shastri.[1] Hangen said that no one else mentioned that name and that his hot favourite was S.K. Patil.[2]

He asked: "Why do you talk about Shastri?"

And I replied: "For the simple reason that he will have the party's support, and ours is a system where the party has to vote for its leader." Mr. Shastri was helped also by the fact that he was so close to my father after Bhubaneswar.

Mr. Shastri was in charge of elections. In the latter period — and I worked very closely with him on that. So when my father was ill, I went to inform Mr. Shastri first of all. I didn't know how much we should say about my father's stroke. I told him that I thought it was very serious, but he did not say that to others, we just said that he was unwell. I also persuaded my father that Mr. Shastri should be closer to him.

*   *   *

I was then Chairman of the Nehru Memorial Trust, but when Mr. Shastri asked me, I accepted the portfolio of the Ministry of Information and Broadcasting. I was very reluctant, though. I had assured Mr. Shastri of my support from the very beginning. In fact, before that, I had got on quite well with Mr. Morarji Desai, although I didn't approve of many of his ideas. But personally or socially, we got on quite well. At that time, Mr. Desai asked for my support, but I had already pledged it to Mr. Shastri.

Most people had given him a vague answer saying: "We are still thinking." My categorical answer angered Mr. Desai.

Mr. Shastri had come to ask for my support. Later he came again. This time he wanted me to be a Minister and he offered me the Foreign Ministry. I did not accept it. In fact, I said I didn't want to be a Minister at all. His reply was that he must have a Nehru in the Cabinet to maintain stability. I pointed out that there was a Nehru who was very anxious to become a Minister and that it was better to choose that person than one who is reluctant. Then I said: "Well, I have a way out. You can say that I have agreed to join the

---

1. He was then Minister without portfolio.
2. Then Congress Party boss of Bombay.

Government but, because I am in mourning, I shall not join now but in two months. By then, you will know whether your position is stable, in which case I won't need to come at all. If there is any difficulty, I will."

I told him also that I would not accept an important Ministry and that my first preference was education. But, since Mr. Chagla[1] was in charge of that office, I thought that he wouldn't want to remove a Muslim. My next choice was Information and Broadcasting. I thought he had agreed to this arrangement. Both my sons hoped that I had not accepted anything; I explained what had happened. We were just talking about it at 8.30 when, on the 9.00 p.m. news, All India Radio announced that I was going to be sworn in with the others. I rang up Mr. Shastri at once. His response was: "I thought it over in the car and felt that your suggestion would create a lot of confusion. Nobody would understand why you should wait for two months. If you are going to join, why not join now?"

This was how I became Minister. I must say, I enjoyed being Minister of Information. I made a lot of changes. But not all of them were seen through to the end.

Neither then nor later did I want to be in the Government. Even now I feel it is a form of imprisonment. It is absolutely untrue to say that my father groomed me for it; because if he had, at least he would have taken me into his confidence about decisions and so on. He didn't. We had discussions but only because I was interested in the subject. Of course, we also had a lot of people to meals and then things were discussed in front of me.

But I would never associate the words fulfilment and leadership together. Government is not my idea of fulfilment. When I see things that are not being done I feel a strong need to do them. This is my attitude. If this room is dirty, I will sweep it. I often wipe this table when I come to the office in the morning because it has not been done properly. This is the argument Mr. Dhebar used when he said to me: "Rather than criticizing things from outside, you should come in and do the job."

---

1. Former Chief Justice of Bombay who became Ambassador to the United States. He was then Minister of Education and subsequently Minister for External Affairs.

Now, this is the problem. Even in the present situation with all these attacks against us, many people want to be leaders but they don't act as leaders. When the Congress is under attack, do they come forward to defend it? Do they speak out boldly? They are part of the Government, but nobody does anything. Therefore, somebody has to do it and this is a situation which was repeated time and again. Now I am rather sorry that I didn't take a more active part earlier, because I could probably have saved my father much unhappiness.

While I say that I didn't want political leadership, I also think that it is not possible for me to be away from problems. Whenever I have been out of India, I have got involved with local problems elsewhere. For instance in Lisbon, on my way from England, I helped to look Jewish girls. That was none of my business, and it wasn't getting me anywhere. But it was a compulsive action. When one sees that something has to be done, or somebody is in need, then one just has to act.

Even though I believe in privacy, and I think I have kept myself a private person in spite of my meeting thousands of people a day, I am always involved in what is happening around me, at any level. Now I happen to be more involved in politics. But there is no doubt that, had I retired in the mountains as I had planned to do, I would have been involved in some of the local problems of the people there. I can't imagine living in isolation.

*   *   *

As for Mr. Shastri, at the beginning, it was said that he lacked decisiveness and that Government policy at that time was some sort of patchwork compromise. This was the recurring theme of Mrs. Pandit's speeches. She also said once that Mr. Shastri was a prisoner of indecision.

I retorted: "You can't be a prisoner of indecision which indicates that the doors are all open to you! You can only be a prisoner of a decision." In the beginning, Mr. Shastri appeared unsure of himself. Whether he really was or not, I don't know, but he always said that after Panditji he was a small man. This gave people a feeling of insecurity. Whoever is leading must be sure that he is the leader. And yet, in the Cabinet, he had declared firmly that, although the opinions of his colleagues were welcome, his word was final. He had said it in no uncertain terms, at the very first meeting. He was probably thinking of Mr. Patil and others who thought they would sway him their way.

At the time of the Pakistani aggression, Mr. Shastri gained self-confidence. I don't think that he really lacked it before. It was only his way of speaking, his style. But, in the beginning, although people admitted his modesty, they wondered whether it was conducive to strength. Then, unfortunately, he had a heart attack soon after he took over.

It was also said that some foreign countries were putting pressure on him. I think that was not fair. The bureaucracy has never been much in favour of non-alignment. They were, and many of them still are, biased in favour of the Western bloc. Mr. Shastri was surrounded by such people.

For instance, when the Soviet Union suggested the Tashkent meeting, Mr. Shastri asked whether the Americans would mind. I remember that I was most distressed at this attitude for I felt that we should not encourage any country to interfere in our affairs.

At some point, I remember warning against the danger of the Congress Party sliding away from the socialist path. I could see that policies were not being implemented and, of course, the more conservative groups had come very much to the fore after my father's death.

*   *   *

Then I went to the USSR in April 1964. I had been made Chairman of the Indian Pavilion for the New York World Fair. As I had never seen an international fair, it was considered advisable that I should see the Moscow one; although it was much smaller, it would give me some idea of how things are displayed.

I had quite a good relationship with Mr. Khrushchev. He used to joke that we had both been Chairmen of our parties. He always talked on that level. Besides, when he and Mr. Bulganin came to India, I was head of the committee in charge of their trip.

Mr. T.T. Krishnamachari led the Indian Delegation to the Commonwealth meeting. I accompanied him. I felt that T.T.K. was not pursuing the foreign policy initiated by my father. I don't know if it was his own choice or whether it was due to his instructions, but I was very unhappy about it.

*   *   *

In October 1964, I was in Paris for the UNESCO Executive Board meeting. One evening, when I was out to dinner, I returned to find several messages from newspaper people. It was about midnight or so and I wondered what on earth had happened. I barely got to my room, thinking I was going to ring back, when one of these chaps — an Indian journalist rang me up and said: "Where have you been? We have been trying to get you; what is your reaction?"

I didn't know what he was talking about. So he told me that Khrushchev had fallen. I was worried as to what reaction it would have on India, whether the Russians would change their policy. Then I got the bright idea that I should go to Moscow.

First, I went to England. Why, I didn't know. I didn't go to meet the High Commissioner. Maybe I had to go to England, anyway. Perhaps I was just going for the weekend for something or other. There, I talked to one or two people and they considered it a good idea. I phoned Delhi. The Foreign Affairs Ministry didn't seem too enthusiastic. But I felt strongly about it. So, I turned to Tito, the one person who I believed would give disinterested advice. Marshal Tito has been closer to India because of the personal friendship between him and my father, because of their very close involvement. They were after all the founding fathers of the non-aligned movement along with Nasser. Between these three there was a special bond and this continued till the end of Nasser's life. President Nasser was always very kind to me. And, so has President Tito been. I naturally thought that the best possible adviser was Marshal Tito — not as a world statesman, but also as a friend. And he has done remarkable things for his country, he has kept Yugoslavia together and given a lead, so I am not surprised that the people show such affection for him. I phoned him. He first said that he was extremely busy as a Head of State was on a visit, but later he said: "Come, I will find time somehow." So my Secretary and I went off to Yugoslavia.

But Belgrade is one of the most difficult places to reach. There was no direct service. We had to change planes in Vienna. P.N. Haksar was our Ambassador there.[1] I only stopped at the airport, but I consulted him. He thought it was a good idea for me to go to Moscow. Tito, too, thought it was a very good idea. I immediately phoned Moscow and said I was coming and that I wanted to see Mr. Kosygin who was the new man at the top. Now, as Tito said, any other country would have made something of the fact that I was the very first person — non-Soviet person — that Kosygin saw. But in India there was no mention of it at all. No mention of the fact that he personally assured me that his policy would remain the same, that he had great respect for my father and that he intended to continue the same policy with Mr. Shastri. External Affairs just thought that it meant nothing at all, and even Mr. Shastri was not at all impressed.

I think that my going to Moscow did a lot of good; I don't know if they would have been quite so friendly had the visit not been made. I had never met Kosygin and I didn't know him at all. He attended my father's funeral, but that was just to express his country's condolences.

My visit to Kosygin at that time was not merely a personal thing; it was very much in the national interest. I started the same kind of relationship with Mr. Kosygin as with Mr. Brezhnev. But it is not true that I went more to the Soviet Union than to America.

Because once a complaint was made in Parliament, I quickly wrote a note to the office asking to find out how many times I had been to each country. It was found that it was exactly equal.

I was extremely well received in the Soviet Union. People ask whether it is a handicap to be a woman: I felt that in the Soviet Union they really wanted to help me, as a sort of younger sister.

* * *

The day I returned from Moscow, the language riots had broken out in South India.[2] Mr. C. Subramaniam, the Union Minister, had resigned. I was discouraged. My immediate reaction was to fly to

---

1. He subsequently became Special Adviser to the Prime Minister.
2. The Constitution of India had provided for the introduction of Hindi as the official language by 1965. In the South, resentment arose against this constitutional provision. The Tamil-speaking people of Madras were particularly incensed. They burned down trains and public buildings. Police fired into the mobs and killed at least sixty people.

Madras. The government said there was no point in going. But I felt very strongly about it and I decided to go on my own if the Government did not wish to send me. And I did. I think my going made a definite difference in calming people.

* * *

A few days later, I was going for a holiday to Srinagar and Mr. Sadiq, who was Chief Minister of Kashmir, was on the same plane. I had heard something about infiltrations from Pakistan but when I had enquired about it I was told that these were mere rumours which should not be taken seriously. Otherwise, I would never have thought of going on holiday at that time.

On the plane Sadiq Saheb said: "I can't convince your people in Delhi, but I think the threat of invasion is more serious than these people are thinking. I don't know how much time we have before the whole thing explodes."

Then he said: "Will you come to dinner tonight and we will discuss it?"

I said: "Look, I am very tired. I am not going to any meal. I am going straight to bed."

Sanjay was with me. At that time, he was very keen on fishing. I said: "He is going out fishing and I am going to bed. From the airport I will go straight to the rest-house to bed and when I get out of bed, I will go straight back to the airport and come back to Delhi. I am not seeing anybody, otherwise it is not a holiday."

I had just finished my sentence when the plane landed. We got down and we saw D.P. Dhar[1] and the entire Cabinet looking as white as sheets. They said: "Well, it is absolute war, and it's here on the outskirts of Srinagar. If you don't do something quickly you can't save us."

They added: "We are having a Cabinet meeting and you have to come."

I was just pushed into the car along with Mr. Sadiq and with far more people than the car could hold. At the meeting they said it was

---

1. He was then Finance Minister in the Kashmir Government. He later became member of the Central Government.

their information that there were large-scale infiltrations and that fighting would start any minute. They added that there were not enough soldiers and not even enough police in Srinagar. So we phoned Delhi and the reply came again that we should not get alarmed. Then, I phoned Mr. Partap Singh Kairon[1] directly and asked whether we could have at least some Punjab police. He was not a man given to niceties and it didn't matter to him whether the government had agreed or whether the Prime Minister had said yes. He simply said yes. I told him that I didn't know what Delhi was going to say about it, but that I thought something had to be done. So he sent some support and, of course, far from resting, nobody went to bed at all. That night we heard firing in Srinagar.

After the Chinese war also I was continuously visiting the front line, and I had established a special rapport with the armed forces.

On 10 January 1966, after signing the Tashkent Agreement which put an end to the 22-day war with Pakistan, Mr. Shastri, "the well-meaning and honest man" who had succeeded my father, hardly nineteen months before, passed away. But there is something I must say about the Tashkent Agreement. It was very unpopular in the country — not the fact that it was an agreement but the terms of it. Knowing how unpopular it was, Shastriji phoned his family and his daughter herself admitted to me later they had told him that the situation would be very tense. In fact, she said that she had scolded and shouted at him.

I was personally upset because, when I went to Haji Pir[2] I had told the cheering soldiers that we would not give it up. The soldiers there had surrounded me and explained how they had fought for it and made sacrifices. But Shastriji seemed to be soft towards the Jana Sangh. I don't know whether I should say "soft". His nature was gentle and some people take gentlemanly and civilized behaviour to mean weakness; they don't see it as a gentlemanly quality. But the common man appreciated it and the nation was plunged in grief at his death. Afterwards, although we had a majority in 1967, Mr. Patil and some others were in favour of a coalition government. When asked

---

1. Partap Singh Kairon was Chief Minister of Punjab.
2. A strategic pass in Kashmir. The Tashkent Agreement included the withdrawal of Indian forces from such strategic places.

how this was possible, they answered: "With the Swatantra Party and Jana Sangh," though both these parties were diametrically opposed to our secularism, our socialism and our foreign policy.

When Mr. Shastri passed away I really didn't think of myself at all. When he had come to ask me to become a Minister I had thought it was just a huge joke and I had told him that firstly, I was not in the mood for jokes, immediately after the death of my father, and secondly that this was a ridiculous proposition. I didn't take him seriously at all. I didn't know that people had been discussing it. I think somebody else had mentioned it to me but again I had dismissed the idea.

Whenever there is a vacancy for anything, they go round to people canvassing. But one does not believe all they say. I must say I was worried at the thought of Mr. Morarji Desai becoming Prime Minister because his policies were so diametrically opposed to what we stood for, and I feared that India would immediately change direction.

CHAPTER 6

The Leader of the Country
The First Phase

On 19 January 1966, nine days after the death of Mr. Shastri, with 67 per cent of the Congress Members of Parliament voting for you (355 votes for you against 169 for Morarji Desai), you were elected leader of the Congress Parliamentary Group.[1]

---

1. It is interesting to recall how the press in India and abroad reported this most eventful day:

   "Mrs. Gandhi is the second woman in history to hold the office of Prime Minister. The first was Mrs. Sirimavo Bandarnaike of Ceylon.

   "As Mrs. Gandhi left the hall of Parliament building where the election had taken place, crowds showered her with flower petals. She kissed many women Members of Parliament, including her aunt, Mrs. Vijayalakshmi Pandit. Earlier, one of the women members had pinned on her shawl a red rosebud like those her father, India's first Prime Minister, always wore in his buttonhole.

   "Security men had to link arms to save Mrs. Gandhi from being knocked over as she passed through the cheering crowds. Many people were pushed into empty ornamental pools . . . .

   "Mrs. Gandhi began her day with a pilgrimage to the shrines of Indian Independence. Early in the morning, she visited the cremation sites of Mahatma Gandhi and Pandit Nehru and the monuments raised in their honour. After having placed offerings and recited prayers, Mrs. Gandhi went to the former residence of her family now transformed into a museum. She stood for a long time in front of a portrait of her father and wept before leaving hurriedly to go to Parliament where the election was to take place.

   "After her election, Mrs. Gandhi called on President Sarvepalli Radhakrishnan at Rashtrapati Bhavan, the presidential palace adjoining Parliament. The President asked her to form a government.

Contd...

On 24 January 1966, you were sworn in as India's third Prime Minister.[1]

"In the evening, at a news conference in the garden of her white bungalow residence at 1 Safdarjang Road, Mrs. Gandhi dressed in a sparkling white sari, with a brown wool shawl draped over her shoulders, stood at a cluster of microphones, answering questions from more than 200 newsmen who trampled her flowerbeds and hedges.

"Although she carefully avoided committing herself to any specific policy, she handled a bristling array of pointed questions with considerable skill. She turned away the silliest and most embarrassing queries with a quip and a smile. To those who asked for her impressions as a woman who had become Prime Minister, she replied curtly, sharply and with evident irritation: 'I do not think of myself as woman in regard to this task. If a woman has the necessary qualifications for whatever profession, she should be allowed to work in that profession.'

"Adding, 'I'm no feminist, I'm a human being. I don't think of myself as a woman when I do my job. According to the Indian Constitution, all citizens are equal, without distinction regarding sex, language or State. I'm just an Indian citizen and the first servant of the country, *desh-sevika.'*

"To a question regarding the fragility of her health inspired by the insinuations of a jealous aunt ('Indira is in frail health indeed'), she replied without hesitation: 'Those who have seen me grow up know that I am both frail and robust. Do you believe that I could have survived if I had a frail constitution? I doubt that you could find anyone who has led as hard life as I have from infancy."

In an article which appeared in the *Look* magazine (30 April 1968) under the title *A Frank Talk With a Powerful Woman*, William Attwood reported: "At the end of her second year in office as Prime Minister, Indira was asked whether being a woman was a handicap or an asset in politics. She answered: "I don't think my being a woman makes any difference at all. It is a question again of putting people in compartments. If you say that this job is only for a man, that man has certain qualities and capacities that a woman does not have. But what are these qualities? Physical strength? No. If you are looking for weak points, you can find them in anybody, and I don't think a person who is head of State should think in terms of himself or herself as belonging to any group. Whether it is sex, religion, or caste, if the people accept you as leader of the nation, that is all that matters."

1. The press reported the ceremony thus:

"Mrs. Gandhi, who wore a white sari with a heavy silver and maroon border, made a solemn affirmation in a clear, quiet voice, repeating the words after Mr. Radhakrishnan.

"A small group of friends who watched the ceremony included Mrs. Gandhi's aunt, Mrs. Vijayalakshmi Pandit, and V.K. Krishna Menon, former Defence Minister. *Contd...*

On 1 March, you made your debut in Parliament as Prime Minister. You promised to review the food policy and to lift the National Emergency which had been in force since 1962. You proposed a new economic programme. In fact the economic situation demanded urgent action. You displayed a spirit of pragmatism married to idealism.

You showed a sense of urgency, prompt action and encouraged cooperation. The Indian rupee was devalued by 36 per cent. But this was an unpopular decision. By taking it you revealed that you could, when necessary, take an unpopular decision.

The Punjab problem was another tricky one in which you were involved by your predecessor. You reached the conclusion that only a linguistic reorganisation could solve it.

On 25 March 1966, you, who were closely identified with your father's thinking on international affairs and who didn't initiate any major departure in foreign policy, started your first foreign tour as Prime Minister.

From 28 March to 1 April, in response to an invitation from President Johnson, you paid an official visit to the United States.[1]

"Mrs. Gandhi went up and kissed Mrs. Pandit before the ceremony, then said laughingly: 'Oh dear, I don't want lipstick marks on me.'

"She stopped to a small table and signed the official papers before witnesses. She wore no earrings, her only jewellery being a wrist watch and a black bead necklace. The only evidence of cosmetics appeared to be the touch of pale red lipstick. Mrs. Gandhi's short bobbed hair was in contrast with the long hair worn by most Indian women."

1. She has gone to the United States almost every year since 1960. After her visit in 1961, Mrs. Lyndon Johnson is reported to have said: "To see India, you must visit the villages. To understand India you must read Tagore. But to know India you must have a teacher like Indira Gandhi. I was lucky because I had all three."

Among published reports on Mrs. Gandhi's visit was one by William White, a columnist of the *Washington Post* who had not been particularly friendly to India. He wrote: "No previous conference of heads of State in the time of the Johnson administration has accomplished so much for so many as has the President's party here with Mrs. Indira Gandhi... It turned out, in short, that she has been and intends to remain a moderate minded, undoctrinaire leader of India — not in our pocket, of course, but also not at our throats."

Contd...

On the way to the United States, you broke journey in Paris; where you met President de Gaulle. On the return journey, you met Prime Minister Wilson, in the course of a brief stop over in London. You also made a halt in Moscow, where you had discussions with Chairman Kosygin.

In 1967 the General Election took place. For the first time you headed the Congress election campaign. During the first two months of the year you toured 15,200 miles and addressed 160 public meetings. You attracted large crowds. One of your biographers wrote on that occasion: "Her obvious aristocratic refinement, which made her an object of awe and admiration for a large number of the Indian masses, was blended with a healthy maternal common sense to which the average housewife could identify. The subtle synthesis of aristocracy and populism was to be the secret of her political success."

After the election, the Congress lost many seats in several States and there were non-Congress governments in some of them. You welcomed the change as a sign of the times and assured the non-Congress Governments of cooperation. At the Centre, the Congress majority was weakened, and in the challenging situation you were unanimously elected leader again. Your position had never been stronger.

I WAS ELECTED LEADER OF THE PARTY ON 19 JANUARY 1966. Morarji Desai chose the date, and I was sworn in as Prime Minister on the 24th. I think Mr. Kamaraj[1] and others supported me just because they felt that I had the majority in the party, between Mr. Morarji Desai and myself. The other person whose name was then mentioned was Mr. Chavan.[2] I offered my support to Mr. Chavan, but he had investigated the situation and thought that I had the majority.

Time made this comment: "The result of Mrs. Gandhi's visit was primarily a new mood of increased warmth and understanding between the United States and India. She and the President decided during the week that they were going roughly in the same direction, and that they could accomplish things without making demands on each other. Mrs. Gandhi proved to be not only "a very friendly, very gracious, and very able lady" as the President called her, "but a fiercely independent ruler with a determination equal to his own."

1. President of the Congress Party.
2. The then Defence Minister.

Mr. D.P. Dhar[1] and some others told me earlier that Patnaik was supporting Mr. Morarji Desai. He had always been close to Mr. Desai and, in fact, of the Orissa group only Nandini Satpathi supported me at that stage. Patnaik went to scold her. She said it was both her private opinion, and one based on ideology. He was quite angry.

Mr. Barooah and some others were discussing the matter when Mr. Patnaik tried to canvas for Mr. Morarji Desai. They told him they were supporting me. He also went to Atulya Ghosh to tell him to support Morarji Desai. But, in the meantime, these people had gone to Atulya Babu who had agreed to support me.

They said: "Will you come with us to her to make her accept that we should propose her name?"

Patnaik had come there, to Atulya Ghosh, and he had talked to Morarji when these people arrived. Then, they all came together to my house and Patnaik told them: "You sit here, I'll call her out."

He came to me and said that he had brought some friends and that they all wanted me to be Prime Minister. Then, I remembered what had happened about the Kamaraj Plan and I told them about it. There was a very strong feeling against Morarji Desai. I think, at that point, they were not so much for me as against him. India's problems were quite serious then — in fact there was a drought — and I think that it was only because I had no experience at all, that I could be bold enough to feel I could take over. Besides, it all happened very fast. There was little time for hesitation.

When I was asked to stand for the Presidentship of the Congress, I was most reluctant because I was sure that I couldn't manage it. I did not have doubts, I was absolutely certain that I wouldn't be able to handle it. All these big people were going to bully me and I would have to answer back. I went to ask for my father's advice. He said: "It must be your decision. I am not going to enter into it."

I learnt that he had been against the idea when Mr. Pant had asked him. But, to me, he didn't say yes or no. Mr. Pant simply said: "It's

---

1. Freedom fighter. A close friend. Later Ambassador to Moscow, Minister for Planning, and Chairman of the Indian Government's Foreign Policy Planning Committee.

not a question of your decision. We have decided and you have to do it. This is your duty."

So, I said yes. Then, I went back to my room and I rang him back immediately saying: "No, Pantji, I have thought about it, I can't do it."

He told me that the news had already gone to the press. Then, of course, all the papers came out with very caustic comments suggesting that my father had pushed me into the job and that I couldn't do it. We all came back from Jaipur to Delhi and, there, I went to Mr. Dhebar and said: "I am quite serious, I simply cannot do it. It is not fair either to me or to the organization."

Mr. Dhebar replied: "Do you really want these newspapers to get away with what they are saying?"

That made me think and I felt that at least I had to show them that I could do it. They had hit a tender spot.

But on this occasion I don't think I really debated at all whether I could do it or not. I really was quite numb after my father's death. I was not thinking about things deeply. And we did have a very difficult period.

* * *

The India of 1966 was facing serious and multifarious problems: unparalled drought, acute food shortage, inflation, official language controversy, demands for Punjabi Suba, problem of the Nagas, Sino-Indian dispute and diplomatic isolation.

In February 1966 at the AICC annual session in Jaipur, the food problem was the dominant issue. The Government was criticized for not implementing the Bhubaneswar resolution on socialism.

On 1 March, I made my debut in Parliament as Prime Minister. I promised to review the food policy and to lift the National Emergency which had been in force since 1962. I proposed a new economic programme. The Indian rupee was devalued by 36 per cent. I encouraged co-operative effort. After the first drought, I ordered stocks to be rushed to Kerala and West Bengal, backed up a programme to import grains and fertiliser, toured the scarcity areas of Orissa, Madhya Pradesh and Maharashtra, and persuaded State Governments to take up extensive relief works and food distribution arrangements. I gave support to a programme of intensive cultivation. There was brisk movement of available foodgrains. A large number of fair-price shops were established. After the second drought, the non-Congress Governments of Bihar, West Bengal and Kerala received all possible cooperation from the Centre. A great crisis had threatened the country and it was overcome. I said at the end of the first period of crisis: "I think we can congratulate ourselves in having come through a most difficult period with minimum distress. I regret that this has so far been unsung, unnoticed."

The decision on the devaluation of the rupee (6 June) was taken not on the World Bank's advice, but because people like Ashok Mehta[1], whom I thought was a good economist, experts of the Finance Ministry, the Cabinet Secretary and our economists said it was a must for India. I personally knew little about the whole thing. I said: "Well, if it is a must, even if it is unpopular, we have to do it."

The Planning Commission also thought it should be done. Had they said no, I would have followed their advice, even against the World Bank's. But the Indian experts opinion was there. Of course, it was the wrong thing to do and it harmed us greatly, because it put up the price of our import — we were still importing quite a lot and it didn't increase our exports very much as it might have if we had been an industrialised country.

Around the same time, I had to make another unpopular decision. It concerned a tricky problem which I inherited from my predecessor: the Punjab problem.

There was a demand for Punjabi Suba, the creation of a Punjabi speaking State. Since Independence, the Sikh community had been pressing for a linguistic partition of the bi-lingual West Punjab State and the creation of a State in which they would predominate.

My father had been strongly opposed to the idea, but, by 1966, the demand had grown so strong that the Centre was in no position to resist it, especially when Sant Fateh Singh — the politico-religious leader of the Akali Dal, the party of militant Sikh nationalism — served notice of his intention to fast to death unless Punjabi Suba was conceded. The Congress found itself in a dilemma: to concede the

---

1. Economist. Leader of the Socialist Party, who was for some time member of Mrs Gandhi's Government.

Akali demand would mean abandoning a position to which it was firmly committed and letting down its Hindu supporters in the projected Punjabi Suba; not to do so would precipitate a Sikh agitation which would certainly turn violent.

I reached the conclusion that only a linguistic reorganisation could solve the Punjabi problem. In response to a personal appeal from me, Sant Fateh Singh agreed to postpone his fast for a month. And then, on 9 March, the Congress Working Committee passed a unanimous resolution in favour of the creation of Punjabi Suba. Unfortunately, Mr. Shastri had made Sardar Hukam Singh, the Speaker of the Lower House, Chairman of the Parliamentary Committee on Punjabi Suba, although he was very biased in favour of Punjabi Suba. It was an extraordinary situation. But I never managed to see Mr. Shastri about this. He was Prime Minister and I was number three after him, and yet in the eighteen months that he was Prime Minister, I could not get a single appointment with him on this. When the Punjabi Suba demand was on, I was very worried and some other people on the Committee were as well. There were three of us. I went to Mr. Chavan and said I had heard that Sardar Hukam Singh was going to give a report in favour of Punjabi Suba and that he should be stopped. Of course, it was up to the Government to take the decision, but once the Prime Minister's appointee had declared himself in favour of Punjabi Suba, how could we get out of it? Every time I would ask for an appointment, Shastriji would say: "Right now we have a meeting. But why don't you stay on after the meeting?"

The meeting would go on for hours, and he would have another appointment or it would be very late. One day, a similar thing happened; one meeting went on till 2.00 or 2.30. That was the time when certain allegations had been made against Krishnamachari[1]. But Shastriji had said that we could stay on and talk to him — all three of us — I don't remember who the third person was. But he just wanted to talk to Krishnamachari and ask him to resign.

I said to Chavan: "If we get out of this room, we are never going to get in again and that report is going to be written any day now; so, I think we should just stick here, however awkward it is for us or for him."

---

1. T.T. Krishnamachari, Finance Minister, was then accused of corruption.

We moved as far to the corner as we could, it was in my other office. The Prime Minister took Krishnamachari to the window and we sat on the other side of the room. We kept talking because we didn't want to eavesdrop. Shastriji just said he was fully in touch with the situation and we needn't bother. So Chavan said: "Look, what is the point in our meeting and our getting het up about it if he is dealing with it? He has met our Committee but he is not bothered about it. And he never asked us whether we would serve or not, he just announced in Parliament that this was the Committee. So, why should we bother?"

But I was very bothered and I went around seeing everybody. Of course, once the report came, it was too late to change it. My view always is that, if there is strong public pressure anything will work. It is not a matter of principles on which one need hold out. Although actually, when the Committee was formed many of the people were very unhappy — even those who had been fighting for it. They suddenly found they had a much smaller area in which to function.

This startling reversal of Congress policy was totally unexpected. While a Sikh agitation had been averted, the Hindu minority in the projected Punjabi Suba felt let down. Communal rioting, instigated by the Hindu revivalist Jan Sangh, erupted in several areas of the Punjab and spread even to Delhi. Mob violence reached its peak when three Congressmen were burnt alive in the town of Panipat near Delhi.

I was very upset when I addressed a civic reception at the Red Fort for the visiting Yugoslav Premier, and said: "There are no tears in my eyes; there is anger in my heart.... Is it for all this that so many freedom fighters and martyrs have sacrificed their lives? How would I hold my head high and say India is a great country and meet foreign dignitaries when violence and discord have fouled the atmosphere?. .. I have a great deal of patience and tolerance, but not beyond a limit. All necessary force will be used to put down internecine fighting. The political parties who are indulging in violence are doing the country great harm. They are not true Indians. Those amongst them who profess to understand Hinduism know nothing about Hinduism."

Nevertheless this bold decision on the Punjab paid off in the next few months. While the Sikhs were delighted with the unexpected concession of their demand, the Hindi speaking population of the Punjab was satisfied with the creation of a new State of Haryana. A dispute over which one of the new States would get Chandigarh, the capital of the former united West Punjab province, was side-stepped by the quick decision to make the city a Union territory.

Two months after assuming office I started my first foreign tour as Prime Minister. From 28 March to 1 April, in response to an invitation from President Johnson, I paid an official visit to the United States. Because of the drought and also because we were getting aid from the USA, Shastriji had planned a visit to the USA in February. Everybody said that I should go, otherwise I would be thought of as anti-American. As I couldn't go in February, I went in March and I enjoyed a very good reception. In fact, the papers even said that no President had ever gone out of his way for a guest as President Johnson had for me. He walked me home to Blair House where I was staying. Once, he came to a reception where he was not expected: our Ambassador had been told earlier that the President never goes to Ambassadors' receptions, that the Vice-President deputizes for him. But President Johnson did turn up. And he wouldn't leave. As he hadn't been invited to dinner, Vice-President Humphrey was the ranking guest and he was to make a speech. As Johnson did not seem to be going, the Nehrus[1] finally asked him if he would stay to dinner.

"Of course I am staying to dinner," he replied.

So, they had to rush and change the table. Vice-President Humphrey was a little put off because he had a beautiful speech prepared but naturally the President had to speak. In spite of all this, President Johnson didn't sign the sanction for the wheat ship to come to India. Meanwhile, we were frantic because we didn't have wheat for the next week. Had we known for sure that we were not getting it, then we would have adjusted, we would have had stricter rationing or something. But, every time we asked the Americans, we were told that the papers were on the President's table.

*   *   *

On my way to Washington, I stopped in Paris where I met President de Gaulle for the second time. I had met him once on a visit to Paris with

---

.. B.K. Nehru, my cousin, who was then Indian Ambassador to Washington, and his wife.

my father. I had found him rather cold and we had not had much conversation. On that trip, though, I found him very considerate. Later, he had a conversation with L.K. Jha[1] and he said: "Politics are very difficult for a woman to manage but I think this one will make it!"

He was a very remarkable person and I admired him tremendously because he wanted to give France its rightful place which I think every country should have. Just because another country is bigger or more powerful why should that give her the right to dominate anyone's national life. And this is what de Gaulle stood for in France. In fact, he wasn't a democrat. He wasn't at all. He had a different vision of France and he implemented his ideas. But I don't think the French are basically democratic. No, they are not. They are very free. It is a free country. It is a country where you have a lot of freedom, but democracy is not very clear in France.

When I came home, I was accused of having turned too pro-American. You see, if you say a good word about America you are immediately accused of being too pro-American. If you say something about the Soviet Union, the Americans immediately accuse you of being a fellow-traveller. I have been very much on my own since I was quite small and have never gone entirely one side or another.

*   *   *

In October 1966, we held the tripartite non-aligned Summit Conference in Delhi, and I tried to revive close contacts with Egypt and Yugoslavia, and to restore the anti-colonial trends of India's foreign policy. Jointly with President Tito and President Nasser, we called for an unconditional halt in the United States bombing of North Vietnam. This and my previous denunciations of the bombing resulted in strained Indo-American relations.

Beside this the main outcome of this tripartite meeting was our collective approach to the economic challenges to non-alignment and peaceful co-existence. The newly independent and developing nations will be liable to strains and pressures until they attain a minimum level of development and enter a stage of self-sustaining growth.

*   *   *

---

1. Principal Adviser to the Prime Minister.

In November 1966, there was a big agitation for ban on cow slaughter[1].

These agitations are very much linked to elections. In between no one seems bothered as to what is happening to the cows or to various other religious matters. Actually a general election was due soon after. Mr. G.L. Nanda was Home Minister. Many of us felt that a procession should not be allowed, but he had great respect for all *sadhus*[2] and proclaimed they would be non-violent, but they weren't.

* * *

In September 1967, I visited Ceylon and in October, I visited Moscow, Poland, Yugoslavia, Romania, Bulgaria and the UAR. In November, I paid a very rushed visit to the Soviet Union again on the occasion of the 50th anniversary of the Russian Revolution.

On 5 September 1967, I took also charge of the Ministry for Atomic Energy, of the Foreign Ministry and of the Planning Commission. I resolutely resisted the demands that India should

1. One of India's problems is the cow population, consisting of about 230 million useless cows. In primitive Aryan societies, the dairy became the temple of worship; perhaps that is how cows became sacred in the old Hindu society and were protected. The campaign for the prohibition of cow slaughter was started by the Jan Sangh. The motive of its members was the desire to strike at the central government, and therefore they did not take up their demands in the States which alone had the constitutional powers for agricultural legislation. Having called on the Government of India to prohibit cow slaughter, the Jan Sangh chose Delhi for demonstrations.

2. So-called holy men, most of whom are ignorant mendicants living on the credulity of the masses. They were brought to Delhi by the Jan Sangh to demonstrate in front of the Parliament House, when the Lower House was in session. Gulzarilal Nanda, the Home Minister, was a believer in the holiness of the *sadhus*. He had accepted the presidency of the Sadhu Sangh. On 7 November, a mob of half-naked yelling *sadhus* carrying tridents, axes and knives burned down cars and government buildings and assaulted individuals. Mrs. Gandhi, who had just returned from a tour of the drought-stricken areas of Bihar, addressed the Lower House. "This is not an attack on the Government," she said. "It is an attack on our way of life." She promised that henceforth violence would be put down with force. The Congress Party demanded the removal of Home Minister Nanda who was replaced by Chavan.

produce an atom bomb in response to China's nuclear programme. My attitude to nuclear disarmament was that any non-proliferation treaty couldn't be one-sided. There should be a balance of responsibilities as between nuclear and non-nuclear nations.

When the Israel-Arab war broke out, I took a firm stand for an end to the aggression by Israel and negotiations on the basis of a pre-war position. I worked to this end at the United Nations.

On Vietnam, as I said earlier, I stood for negotiations and the cessation of US bombing of North Vietnam as a preliminary stage.

I worked in the spirit of the Tashkent Agreement and reaffirmed India's goodwill to Pakistan. I expressed our willingness to discuss all problems between the two countries in a friendly spirit, if Pakistan was willing.

China's attitude was still unfriendly and she has made threatening moves against India, but India has been patiently waiting for China to open a dialogue in appropriate conditions.

*   *   *

Inaugurating the Second UNCTAD Conference in New Delhi, I said: "We are conscious that we bear the mark of the storms we have weathered. I hope you will also recognize the spirit of the country, a spirit, which has seen our people through countless difficulties, natural calamities and man-made complexities. It is this spirit that has inspired our great men through the ages. Some of our problems are centuries old, and some are very new — parched land and bursting cities, illiteracy and brain-drain.

I drew the attention of the Conference to the gap between rich and poor nations. I said: "Today the rich nations find it more rewarding to invest their savings in their own security, in the advance of their own technology, or even in establishing contacts with distant planets. They find it more interesting to trade amongst themselves than with the developing nations. Their markets and profit patterns are protected by tariff and non-tariff barriers. The efforts of the less developed countries to process their natural products and increase their share of international trade in manufacture and processed goods are thus frustrated."

The continuous onslaught of synthetics and substitutes further deprive poor nations of the resources they would devise from the use of their products. Thus the gap keeps growing.

The last year of the Third Plan had suffered from the effects of drought, of aggression from across the borders and by a pause in the aid from outside. Uncertainty about domestic and external resources delayed the preparation of the Fourth Plan and there was a spirited debate on the size of the Plan. I told the Planning Commission: "The lower we aim the less we shall achieve.... We must think of the Plan in physical terms and in terms of the minimum needs if we are to convince the people that life is worth living.... We must have realism, yes, but realism in regard to whom and what? If we do not have a feeling for the people, then why plan at all? I do not decry aid if it helps us to stand on our own feet."

The two droughts and the industrial recession forced a postponement of a new five-year plan, although planning was continued in the form of annual plans.

* * *

It is in such circumstances that the 1967 election took place. For the first time I was heading the Congress election campaign. During the first two months of the year I toured 15,200 miles and addressed 160 public meetings, attracting large crowds.

I think that what appeals to the masses is sincerity. If they feel that a person, whatever the faults, is genuinely making an effort, that is what counts.

Perhaps the manner in which I spoke counted. But I am not an orator. Even if I wanted to be one, I couldn't. After the election, the Congress lost many seats in several States and there were non-Congress Governments in some of them. I welcomed the change as a sign of the times and assured the non-Congress Governments of co-operation. At the Centre, the Congress majority was weakened, and in the challenging situation I was unanimously elected leader again. With the Congress in power in some States, there was a change in Centre-State relations.

Democracy implies choice. Choice involves alternatives. It is a sign of health when alternatives are emerging and competing. Unfortunately, they didn't really emerge because in these coalition governments, the range of parties getting together was so wide, or the opinions were so divergent that they couldn't really concentrate on any actual work or development. Except in Bengal where there was a Communist Government. There, the quarrel came up on other matters. But policy-wise there was not that same divergence. In most other places, our opponents did nothing about some of the problems which they had always accused the Congress of neglecting and about which later they said we were not doing enough. But, during their own period in power, nothing was done.

In a place like Bihar, for instance, there was a communal riot. The first one erupted in an industrial complex, at Ranchi, in the public sector. The Jana Sangh was a member of the local Cabinet. When I visited the area the Chief Minister had a Cabinet meeting to discuss the matter with me. But he gave a different timing to the Jana Sangh Ministers. The others told me quite openly: "We are sure that the Jana Sangh are behind this riot and that is why we haven't asked them now and we want to say something quickly before they come in half an hour."

How can you work together in such conditions? And this has continued to happen. I think that it is largely because none of them had a programme. They have accused us of being populist but they are the ones not to have put out a programme and gone to the people to say: "This is our programme and we will stick by it whether we win or lose."

This is a position that I have taken even lately, for instance with the inflation when we took drastic measures. Some of my colleagues asked me whether I realized that, with such a policy, we couldn't win the next election.

I said: "Well, all right, we may lose the next election but we cannot say that we will let the economy deteriorate now so that we win the next election."

It has always been my policy. Many choices would have been much easier for me to make so far as I personally was concerned. Even at the time of the split in the Congress, all I had to do was to go along with it. But I didn't think this was the right thing for the country and therefore I stood out and I think this is what the people respect. At that time I had no idea that the majority would be with us, and neither did I know how the people would react afterwards when we took steps against inflation, or even with the emergency. It just had to be done. If they didn't like it we would have to face the consequences.

CHAPTER 7

The Leader of the Country
The Second Phase

On 12 March 1967, you again became Prime Minister. Although the general elections had led to a temporary closing of ranks within the Congress, keen interparty competitions had started. In 1951, Mr. Nehru had decisively broken the independence of the party organisation and established his supremacy. But in 1967 there was instability in various States and a sort of trial of strength started between the Congress and you.

On 20 August 1969, the split in the Congress actually took place. On 31 October, a rival session of the Congress Working Committee took place at your residence, and on 12 November you were asked to quit the Indian National Congress. On the same day, you went to Paris to attend the funeral of General de Gaulle.

The Heads of State of the entire world were assembled In Notre Dame to pay a last tribute to the man who incarnated France for so many years. What were your thoughts? Did you meditate upon the certain similitude of the two destinies which rejoined across the centuries that of Joan of Arc?

The Congress split became a fact. This event revealed your unsurpassed personal potential. It showed that you were as skilful in dealing with seasoned colleagues and rivals as you are apt at handling crowds. So far as the country was concerned, you were the dominant figure. All the other people had come and gone. It seemed that you had reached the same heights as your father.

On 1 March 1971, the country went to the polls again. It was
an extraordinary electoral campaign that you conducted. It had
been said that "what has been extraordinary and exhilarating is
that the elections became a sort of movement — a people's
movement."

WHEN I WAS RE-ELECTED LEADER OF THE CONGRESS, AND therefore Prime Minister, on 12 March 1967, I was determined not to let my public life deprive me of the things that make life worth living. And I said so to the press at once. First you find these things outside yourself and then, as you grow older, I think you find most of them within you. For lack of time, I have given up most of the outside ones, although, even now, I try to go to exhibitions and so on. When Delhi held its first International Book Fair,[1] I spent four hours there, on two different days have been to almost every art exhibition but I have hardly been to any concerts because you can't leave it in the middle, because of an urgent summons. I can only go to a performance where this is possible. At a music recital, it is somehow impolite to the musicians if you drop in and don't take it seriously. But I wouldn't say that I have given up music because, as I said, somehow you find it within you. I don't know how to explain it. In a way, it is because I don't separate work from relaxation. To me it is the same, just different aspects of the same life. Most politicians get very tense because they are playing a part, they are putting up a front. I am not, I am just me as I am. If I enjoy doing a thing I do it. This is why I am never anxious.

* * *

Although the 1967 general elections had led to a temporary closing of ranks within the Congress, keen interparty competitions had started. The four years which followed were a period of acute instability in several States. However, I initiated moves to lighten the rigours of the Emergency Regulations promulgated after the Chinese aggression in 1962 and ordered the relaxation of the Gold Control Rules.

---

[1]. In 1976.

I took the responsibility for the release of Sheikh Abdullah from detention in the hope that he would work for peace in Kashmir, and for friendly relations between India and Pakistan.

I made a strenuous effort to reconcile the aspirations of the hill people in Assam with the needs of the administration and of the integrity of the country.

I restarted parleys with the rebels in Nagaland.

Because I believed that groups and tribes living in hill areas had been neglected, I took deep interest in plans for the development of hill regions. I initiated measures to increase production, by releasing it from cumbersome administrative regulations. I associated people from outside the administrative establishment with consultation and decision-making. It is on one of these occasions (The Round Table on Tourism) that I said: "We have a tendency to regard ourselves as morally superior to others. This does us no good."

I told public sector managers: "The public sector must stand or fall, like the private sector, on the tests of efficiency, profit, service and technological advance."

I exhorted the public sector to set an example of self-reliance: "We should not go in for turn-key jobs or seek foreign collaboration the second or third time. Our engineers, scientists and technicians are second to none. Government has been too cautious and conservative in giving them greater opportunity to show their work."

In my convocation address at the University of Roorkee, on 18 November 1967, I said: "Science fights superstition. The unquestioning reverence of everything old is superstition. The notion that some races or religions or castes are superior to others is a superstition. The belief that a system of thought appropriate to one historical situation is of universal validity is a superstition. Science, on the other hand, is attuned to change. For various reasons, superstition is entrenching itself and finding new supporters. Without the help of science, I see little hope of checking the virus of religious hatred. Scientists and technologists should make it their mission to spread the scientific temper so that our forward march is not blocked by obstacles of superstition."

*   *   *

In 1967, a sort of trial of strength started within the Congress. Th: ˅ tried on me the same sort of thing as they had tried with my fatɩ…. When they considered that somebody was close to me, they would attack that person rather than me. The person may not really have been close to me, that was immaterial, until it became obvious that he was not. Then he was alright, he would become a good person and so on. This is the sort of thing that has been going on, although now they all say that they approve of my basic policy, whether they believe it or not I don't know; but publicly this is their line, and then they accuse me of not implementing that policy.

Some claimed that the Congress should formulate policies and supervise their implementation by the Government. But I and my colleagues in the Government resisted this claim on the ground that the Government, which had a wider responsibility to Parliament and the country, could not accept such limits to its independence. I was very careful to avoid being identified with any faction, but I had to show flexibility as there was nothing to gain by precipitating a split in the Congress Party. It would have been harmful to the country. There were smaller splits but I felt that a major one would weaken the Congress, and the Congress was the only party which was a national party and whose ideas and philosophy could hold the country together. So, I was worried and I think I went to very great lengths to avoid it.

A challenge emerged on the occasion of the elections of the Union President and Vice-President. When Dr. Zakir Husain was selected as our candidate a lot of our people didn't like the idea of a Muslim becoming President. It was the first time. But, when I stuck to it, they supported me on it. Then they said that he was a bad choice not because he was a Muslim but because he wouldn't win. That was the excuse. So I said: "Let's lose but we should still try."

And, of course, he won.

I think it was a great thing because it broke the chain. For instance, before that, Fakhruddin Sahib[1] was Finance Minister in Assam and every now and again someone would say that he should be Chief Minister but that, as he was a Muslim, he just couldn't be chosen.

---

1. He later became President of India.

After Dr. Husain's election, we have had Muslim Chief Ministers in Hindu majority States and in other important positions.

Nevertheless, after the 1967 election, there was definite split in the Party. It was not obvious to all, but it was obvious to us, to everybody here, because every time we had a meeting of the Executive of Parliamentary Party, there would be tension and some people would deliberately try to — I won't say insult, although it was pretty near — but needle me on any small point and make it as unpleasant as possible. Mr. Patil was openly saying that we should have a coalition government. We asked him whom with. He said Jana Sangh and Swatantra. Two parties whose policies, foreign and domestic, had always been diametrically opposed to the Congress's since the very beginning. So this difference was there and it was growing.

It was in the sphere of foreign affairs actually that the first signs of ideological polarisation appeared. During the Arab-Israel war of June 1967, I came out against Israel as the aggressor, and Mr. Morarji Desai's visit to Japan and the USA provoked an open clash. I don't think he would have done anything by himself, but his followers kept on saying that he had their full support and that he should not knuckle under me and that sort of thing. Sucheta Kripalani[1] and Ashok Mehta played a part in this. Of course, Sucheta wanted very much to be in the Government and perhaps things would not have come to such a head if she had been. But then she didn't really approve our policies. She was very pro-West and she had been strongly opposed to my father on account of her husband and also, I think because of her own inclination.

*   *   *

In July 1968, there was the famous case of supply of arms to Pakistan and also the Soviet Union's invasion of Czechoslovakia. India did not vote for the West-sponsored United Nations resolution and internally this led to a lot of discussions. Factional warfare in the Congress escalated rapidly. And then, in April 1969, at the Faridabad Congress

---

1. A Congress leader of Uttar Pradesh. Acharya Kripalani, her husband, was a veteran Congress leader, companion of Nehru, Gandhi, etc., who subsequently left the Congress Party.

Session two rival points emerged on virtually every issue. It happened in a very strange way. Traditionally, the Congress President always shows the Prime Minister the written speech he will deliver at the Congress Committee meeting. All Congress Presidents used to show it to my father. I know this because, quite often, they would give it to me and ask me to have him glance through it and give it back to them. But it is not a rule. They don't have to. So, Mr. Nijalingappa, the Congress President, didn't show his speech to me and it never struck me that I should ask for it. In fact, I didn't ask Barooah, the current President of the Congress Party, for the speech he delivered at the last session. I spoke in the morning, extempore, without any notes. I outlined what I thought was the Congress policy, and then, in the afternoon, Nijalingappa said exactly the opposite. He read his written speech.

The battle was reopened in May with the death of Zakir Husain. I had chosen Zakir Husain, not because he was a Muslim, not because I liked him, but because I had spoken to a large number of Members of Parliament, Members of Legislative Assemblies and other people and they had all said that there was nothing against him except his religion. Many had supported him even though he was a Muslim; but those who were against him had admitted that their only reason for it was his religion. It seemed to me that opinion was almost unanimous in his favour. When he died, once again, I started talking to people. I never tried to impose my choice. I would simply say: "Some names have been mentioned in the newspapers, you have seen them. What would you like to say about them?"

I met nearly all the opposition leaders too. I got the impression that they all supported Giri, the Vice-President. So far all the Vice-Presidents had become Presidents and although it doesn't mean that we should always stick by this precedent, there was no real reason to bypass Giri. Morarji was the only person who honestly said that he didn't support him, although Giri had been chosen Vice-President at his special request. I had accepted him then because I thought that it made it easier for Zakir Husain to become President. Therefore I was very surprised when Morarji said he didn't want Giri. He was the only one to say so quite frankly. When I asked them, all the others — whether it was Kamaraj or Nijalingappa — were "thinking about it" or "discussing the matter". Then I started asking people: "Suppose for some reason we can't have Giri, the second name I propose is that of the Agriculture Minister, Mr. Jagjivan Ram."

So, when they chose Sanjiva Reddy, I was upset because some people who I thought — I may be mistaken — had said they would support Giri, voted for Reddy at the meeting. The score was six to five. Moreover it was very wrong for a Parliamentary Board to choose the President. Never before had this happened. The choice was always discussed in the Working Committee and so on, because whoever is elected does not simply become the President of a party, he is the President of India.

This was the first time that the Parliamentary Board had selected the President in that way — at least so far as I know. When Reddy won the vote there, I decided to support him too; I thought I would go along and, therefore, I signed the paper for his nomination. After that though, they openly said that the point of getting Reddy elected was to get rid of the Prime Minister. A newspaper even carried a signed article to this effect. I felt this was against our very system. The way to remove a Prime Minister is not to create a conflict between the President and the Prime Minister. Our system simply cannot work with such conflict. The decision must be made by the Party. If the Party loses its confidence in him, then the Prime Minister goes.

But even when the conflict came out in the open, I did not wish to tell a single person to vote for Mr. Giri. People, including ministers, did come to ask me what to do. My reply was that they knew the situation and that they had to judge and see for themselves what was the right action.

I did not give such directives. There was talk about the judiciary being aborted into politics but, when Dr. Zakir Husain stood for presidentship, all the opposition was supporting the ex-Chief Justice. With Mr. Sanjiva Reddy, they wanted to change the system through the backdoor by using the President who, under the Constitution, has no such powers.

*   *   *

On 16 July 1969, I wanted to change Mr. Desai's portfolio. So, he resigned from the Cabinet and I took over the Finance Ministry, and on 19 July, 14 major banks were nationalized. The country supported our policy. Mr. Desai had made it clear in Bangalore at the All India Congress Committee where that resolution was adopted that, while he was Finance Minister, there would be no nationalization. Since the Party voted overwhelmingly for nationalization, it seemed to me that there was no other way.

On 20 August, Mr. Giri was elected President of India. The questions clearly at stake were whether *(a)* the Congress should be a mass based organisation or one manipulated by a handful of party bosses, *(b)* it should adhere firmly to its declared policy of secularism and socialism, and *(c)* in a democracy the elected head of government could be overruled by a party organisation which is not responsible to Parliament.

On 31 October, a rival session of the Congress Working Committee took place at my house. There was an exchange of letters — a Correspondence War it was called — and on 12 November I was asked to quit the Indian National Congress. On that very day I had to dash to Paris to attend the funeral of General de Gaulle.

Six days later I sent an open letter to the members of the Congress Party where I explained my views and position.

During this struggle, some people started measuring my actions by my father's standards. I don't like these comparisons. I think that whatever we have been able to do in India is because of the foundations which our leaders laid. My father formulated the policy and laid the foundations of modern India. All we are trying to do is to implement it. A famous quote from Corneille came to my mind at that time: "A qui venge son père, il n'est rien d'impossible." Something of that spirit was there, in the beginning at least, because I did feel I had to vindicate his stand and politics.

* * *

A country's foreign policy cannot be divorced from its internal policy. Any country, any government, any political party must decide what it believes in, and all its policies must then flow from this basic conviction or belief. What is our foreign policy? Some people take the word "non-alignment" to represent the whole of our foreign policy. In a way we are not so attached to the word "non-alignment" as to what it stands for, namely, we believe in judging all issues independently. We do not wish to be tied to any group or to any country.

We are getting closer and closer to the twenty-first century. But unfortunately we find that in large portions of the world, the basic thinking is still very much that of the nineteenth century. The world has changed, we helped change it because of India's freedom movement, because of India's gaining independence and other countries in Asia and Europe becoming free. This has been the greatest change in the world. Although it was obvious to us that we would become free and that our freedom would lead to the freedom of other countries, this process came somewhat as a shock to the colonial powers.

For some time they seemed to be stunned by that shock, but it has not taken them long to recover. And since then, we have seen another very subtle change coming over the world, a rather dangerous change: colonialism — open, frank, honest colonialism — has given way to a veiled neo-colonialism. This has actually happened in some places and in other places there have been attempts at it.

Therefore, the difficulties before the developing countries are still considerable. And to face them we need more than mere idealism, or mere sentimentalism, we need very clear thinking and hard-headed analysis.

Some say that non-alignment has not served our purpose or that it has not been a success. But what is the alternative? Alignment? If we should be aligned, then with whom? The two major blocs are what are commonly known as Eastern and Western blocs. To which should we be aligned? Alignment itself has had many cracks in the last few years in both blocs.

I am sure anybody who looks clearly at this picture will immediately come to the conclusion that it would not be in our interest to join any bloc. Therefore, we come back to the third position, which is outside of blocs. I do not think it is an idealistic position. I think it is the only hard-headed, practical path that is open to any country which wants to keep its independence.

Many of those who have been against non-alignment all these years and who criticized my father and me for trying to pursue this path no longer attack non-alignment as such, but allege that we are not truly non-aligned. The attack today, the sharpest weapon used against our foreign policy, is to allege that in effect we are following the Soviet line. Perhaps they think their saying so will frighten us into abandoning our friendship with the Soviet Union. Perhaps they think that they will be able to blur the independent image which we have gained with our own people and in the world. Let us be very clear that, regardless of what many of our newspapers write, the image of India is of a country standing or trying to stand squarely on its own feet. This does not mean that people always believe us to be right. Many countries point out our mistakes. And on many occasions we ourselves do. On many occasions when we have supported Western countries, the Eastern group has criticized us and interpreted it as weakness. Similarly, when we supported the Soviet Union, or more likely the African-Asian group of countries, the Western world has attacked us.

On one occasion, the American Ambassador to the U.N. complained to me that we had supported the Soviet Union on many more occasions than we had supported other countries. The remark was made at a party and I did not have details with me. But I did know that these were on issues in which India and the developing countries were vitally interested. And if this were so, would it not be more true to say that the Soviet Union had supported the stand taken by the developing countries, by the African and Asian countries, than to state that we had gone out of our way to support the Soviet Union? Afterwards, I put this question to the Ministry of External Affairs and actually when we counted up, we found that it was not even true to say that we had voted with the Soviet Union on more occasions than we had voted with other countries. Even the basic point which the Ambassador had made turned out to be incorrect.

*   *   *

India has always supported the U.N. It is not an ideal organization, but no world organization can be. What I have always said is that if you didn't have the U.N. you would have to have some other world body. There is no escape from some forum where everybody can meet. You may quarrel, you may obstruct the work but nevertheless you need some place where people can meet and discuss and make a serious attempt to solve the problems. Whether you actually solve them or not, is not important, but at least the forum is essential and the U.N. agencies are doing good work.

For instance, I found UNESCO very interesting although so much time went speechifying. I thought UNESCO has an important role to play; it has taken up some very useful projects and done a great deal in the field of education, the preservation of art treasures. But I haven't kept up in touch with the later developments.

We have believed — and we do believe now — that freedom is indivisible, that peace is indivisible, that economic prosperity is indivisible. And these are the fundamentals on which our policy is based, both inside the country and outside. We have stood for the freedom of all countries. Even when we were not free, when we were in no position to help other countries, we went out of our way to give them whatever moral and other support we could. And I know that that moral support was welcome and helped them. Today our position is the same. We know that joining forces with the Afro-Asian group is not immediately going to strengthen the countries of Africa and Asia who belong to that group. But we know that in the long run this is the only way. We share common problems, common difficulties, common threats. And we can face them only by trying to stand on our own feet, by having stability within our countries and by having economic progress. We can have stability and progress only if we take a particular economic path — the path of socialism through which we give social justice to our people. If we stand for social justice in the international sphere, we also believe that, as long as there are poor nations and rich nations, there is bound to be tension.

The tension is not only between the poor and the rich, but also among the rich because of their desire to control or to influence the developing nations. This has been the cause of most wars in the past and this accounts for much of the tension today. Yet, in spite of the difficulties some countries do pursue the path which we have advocated, the path of conciliation, of trying to solve problems by means of negotiation rather than by conflict.

Recent history provides us with two good examples of that policy. No two countries could have fought more bitterly than the Soviet Union and Germany. There have been many wars, but I do not think any has been fought with such great bitterness as the one which took place between these two countries. In Stalingrad, the fighting was not merely nation to nation, not even province to province, it was house to house, almost a fight for each brick of the city. Perhaps you still remember that while the men were fighting, the women were picking up the bricks to show that Stalingrad was determined to survive and build. What tremendous feeling and personal involvement there was among the people! And yet these two countries have been able to come to an agreement to try and solve their difficulties through talking about them openly, forgetting the hatred which went so far back into history. Similarly, negotiation has now been accepted generally as the only possible method of solving the problem of what we call Western Asia and what, in the Western world, is called the Middle East.

Foreign policy has to be based on one's historical and geographical backgrounds. In other words, we see the world from where we stand. Each country sees the world from where it is located. So we cannot possibly have exactly the same angle. Certain countries are our neighbours. So our relationship with them is especially important. If we are a long way from other countries, we can look at them from different angles.

We also find that in devising the foreign policy of any country — and perhaps especially that of India — certain intangible elements can be extremely important or decisive. It may be easier for a rich and powerful nation to press forward its policy and to fashion relations with other countries. India is neither rich nor powerful, and we have to keep that in mind. Nevertheless we have made up for our lack of riches and power with some other qualities.

Earlier, because we were in the forefront of the freedom struggle, we enjoyed a certain influence. We also had leaders of stature who were able to give inspiration to other countries in a position similar to· our own. That situation has changed. These countries have been free for a number of years; they are all attempting to develop their own personalities and none of them would like to be guided by others. They would like to have friends, but they would not like to feel that any one country is superior to them. We would not like that either. So we can understand the sentiments of other countries — and especially smaller countries. We should be very careful at all times not to give an impression of wanting to take a dominant position.

*   *   *

Right now, we find ourselves in an extremely difficult economic and political situation. We should either stand firm on our convictions and make a tremendous effort to strengthen ourselves or try for strength through alliances. As I have pointed out, some people believe there is greater safety in alliances. In my opinion such borrowed strength cannot be enduring, and the feeling of security would be rather deceptive. It would make us complacent and could lead us into dangerous situations later on. The only real security is to strengthen our own people and to be confident of ourselves.

I mentioned intangible elements. By these I mean conviction, courage and national pride. And I would not like anybody to think that the pride which I have in view is the very narrow minded chauvinism which is sometimes displayed by those who imagine that national pride consists in getting offended or feeling insulted at the slightest provocation. Only a weak nation lacking self-confidence feels insulted by other people. As I once said in Parliament, nobody can be degraded except by his own actions; no country can be degraded except by the behaviour and action of its own people. And being poor or weak in the way we are poor and weak is not degrading. It is not a good thing and we must change the state of affairs. But it is not a degrading thing in itself. If, because of our poverty, our economic condition and our lack of military or other strength we were to allow ourselves to abandon our national interest, that would be degrading.

What are we doing? We are striving. Slowly perhaps, but step-by-step over the years we have strengthened ourselves not only in the military sense but also in the economic field. Further, in all international forums we have stood by our convictions, regardless of consequences. That is why we are respected. Nobody will think ill of us because of our understandings with some smaller countries even if we do have some difference of opinion with them. On the contrary, people will blame us for trying to throw our weight about, or trying to pressurise small countries when we disagree with them. In all such matters national interest and national honour must come first, but we must not confuse this with any narrow chauvinistic attitude.

A British statesman said that no country is a permanent foe or a permanent friend. All countries must try to be on good terms with as many others as possible. Our policy is to strengthen existing friendships, to change indifference into friendship, and wherever hostility exists to lessen it. Sometimes it is asserted that India has no friends. This is indeed a strange statement. What is the measure for friendship? Is it a count of countries that would help us in a war? How many countries, whom we call friendly, would really be able to help? The fact is that India, today, has about as many friends as any other country. How we keep our friends does not depend merely on how we act, but also on what happen to be their national interests at any given time. If it is in their interest to be friendly, they will be so, but, if they believe their national interest lies elsewhere, they will not be our friends no matter what we do. So, while we must try to multiply our friendships, we must always be prepared for situations when, conversely a hostile one may decide for various reasons to become our friend. Our attitude must be flexible in these matters.

At no time does it help to speak ill of a country. If there are strong reasons, let us take some steps. But if we do not consider such action desirable, it hardly serves any useful purpose merely to shout. Even the big powers say that war should be avoided. But situations have been created when even a big army, with all its power and influence, has not been able to save them from a mess. Basic conviction and belief in certain principles cannot change. That is a constant feature of both domestic and foreign policy.

Courage and conviction must be allied to an astute, hard-headed analysis of international affairs and events. At all times this analysis has to be devoid of emotion or sentiment. The growth of military power in the hands of a few countries is producing its own antithesis. Nations with military stockpiles of unimaginably destructive potential are unable to use that power. One gun-boat could do much more in olden times than what very much greater arsenals are able to do today, because of the fear of the consequences of using them.

We are friends of the United States and the USSR as well as of many other countries. We are getting help from many of these countries but we have tried not to be dependent on any of them. My government did not yield to any pressures. We didn't find it a problem except that we found that an entirely wrong image of India was projected. That was the only way in which they could retaliate. They couldn't make us change our policy by threat or pressure or cajoling or any other way. The only other way of retaliating was to spread an entirely erroneous and false picture outside. What we were interested in was not India being a leader or being dominated in Asia. On the contrary, we did our best in international forums to encourage the smaller countries. We always proposed the same of Sri Lanka or Nepal, Afghanistan, Bangladesh and so on. So nobody would think that being big in size we were pushing ourselves. But we did, of course, stand firmly by what we considered to be our hard principles and objectives which is that each country should be truly free, strong in itself, free to develop as it wishes. We have tried to buy our essential goods from different countries, and, at the same time, to become self-sufficient and stand on our own feet. But in today's world no country can be absolutely independent of another. It is a world of interdependence. One can be interdependent only if one is secure in one's freedom. If one gives up part of one's freedom, the relationship changes; it is no longer interdependence; it becomes something else, a form of colonialism creeps in. In earlier times people or groups were very much more self-sufficient. They could produce everything they needed and they were content with what they could produce. Each community was a complete sort of unit. Today, it is not so. Each city is dependent on other cities, each State is dependent on other States. This is the situation in the world at large. We may have to get some necessary products from the developed countries, but the developed countries, in turn, cannot exist without a great deal of goods from other countries. We have to see that the relationship is such that it cannot force us into a position contrary to our interests. This is where we have to be firm. That is why we want to be self-reliant in all essentials so as not to be let down or forced to yield to pressure at a time of danger. Until now we have avoided such a position and shall continue to do so.

Although we get many essential products from other countries, at no time has this forced us to change our policy in any manner whatsoever. We have adhered to our conviction and the world has respected us for it. When the United States or the Soviet Union help us by means of financial credits — which are wrongly called "aid" — or by enabling us to produce industrial and defence equipment, we presume that they do it out of their own national self-interest. But our own national interest compels us to build up our economic and defence strength with the help of whoever is prepared to give it and to

At Moscow with Nikita Khrushchev and Andrei Gromyko in 1963

With Prime Minister Lal Bahadur Shastri (1964)

Indira being sworn in as Prime Minister by President Radhakrishnan

Addressing a gathering in Uttar Pradesh

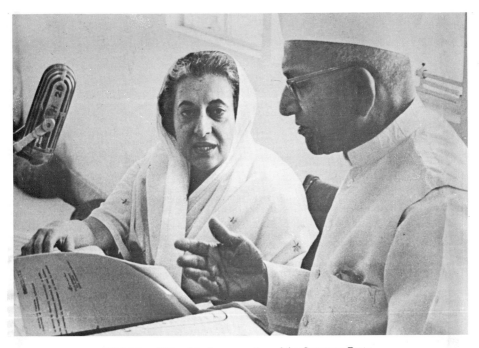

With Morarji Desai during a meeting of the Congress Party

Indira being felicitated by her supporters after her election to the Lok Sabha
was upheld by the Supreme Court in November 1975

On a visit to an outlying military post in Kashmir

Indira being received by members of the Bangladesh Cabinet at Dacca in March 1972

assist us stand on our own feet. Therefore, we will not allow ourselves to be carried away either by anti-Soviet hysteria or by anti-America hysteria.

*   *   *

I always found my visits to the USA very stimulating. There is so much dynamism there, a lot of new ideas, innovations, in every sphere: architecture, dance, music and so on.

I met President Kennedy twice. First when I went with my father and later when I went on a lecture tour. He especially came back from a holiday to give me time because his wife was at that time staying in our house here and she had cabled to him that he should look after me; so, he was specially kind. Even though it was a purely private visit he had sent someone from the Protocol to be with me.

President Johnson was an extremely friendly personality, although he didn't help with grains or anything.

*   *   *

About the Conference of Non-aligned, the question has frequently been asked: "What good can such a conference be and what do we hope to get out of it?" I personally think that the very fact of meeting a large number of Heads of State and sharing experiences with them is useful. While we try to keep in touch with people through letters and through our embassies, this cannot replace personal contact and discussions that take place not only in the forum of the Conference, but individually and informally. This by itself would be a very important reason for holding such a conference.

It is amazing to see that when the non-aligned Asian and African nations get together, some newspapers dig out words like "jamboree" and "picnic" and yet, when other nations get together, those words are never used. Instead, they write they have a "serious meeting" or a "common problem". As if we did not have common problems! What is more amazing is that even when all their predictions turn out to be wrong, they do not hesitate to continue along the same way. I hope nobody is taken in by this kind of comment or reaction.

This is typical of the double standards practised by the West and perhaps by all the countries. When they had the deciding vote at the UN, they didn't think it was wrong. They could bulldoze the others. But when the others get the majority, now, they call it a misuse of majority although they do everything in their own interest whereas the others did everything in their interest. The only difference is that now there is a much larger portion of the world that is covered by developing countries. They have one standard for judging countries whose regimes they approve of and it has nothing to do with the system; it can be an authoritarian system; it can be a dictatorship, benevolent or military; but if they approve or they are on their side, they have only one way of judging them or presenting them. If they don't approve of them, there is another problem.

You see the same in the question of the press and media. This was not all against the Western press. It was a very positive aspect to it which was that in the press of all developing countries there is very little news about ourselves. We have little news about Africa and Asia; but they have also no news about other Asian and African countries. The main purpose was that if there was a link up and there was a news service linking the developing and the non-aligned world we have a much bigger and better coverage of what is happening and are more in touch among us.

The question is even if it is government news but we know what is happening in our countries. Secondly, I don't think that the Western press is as free as is made out. It is influenced by governments some-time, but it certainly is influenced by various powerful and dominant groups or one section and another. Every newspaper has its policy and it does not allow anything against this policy, so it is a question of degree of freedom.

We know that the allied countries are not very happy with the non-aligned group. Neither of them like it. Most big powers would like to have spheres of influence. Although we are very friendly with them, we do not agree with this attitude of theirs and we are certainly not going to help them develop their spheres of influence. The only sphere of influence we want is one of friendship and of mutual help, and I think that in conferences of non-aligned countries, there is much scope for mutual help especially in the economic field. It is not easy because, although many problems are similar, conditions are different and there are all kinds of pressures. But if we are able to help one another to a small extent even to understand the pressures, these conferences will serve a useful purpose. We meet to reinforce our economic and political independence and to tell the world that we want to throw our weight in favour of peace. We do not want a balance of power in favour of power, but in favour of peace. Through friendship it is possible to out-manoeuvre hostility. Indian history indicates that this, indeed, is the sum total of our tradition from the days of the Buddha and the Emperor Ashoka right down to our times of Mahatma Gandhi and Jawaharlal Nehru. These great personages have showed us the essence of our tradition and Gandhiji specially brought it out from the safe-keeping of an ideal into the very business of daily living, the hurly-burly of political and economic policy. It would be a grave mistake to give this up for what may be considered to be a temporary gain as some of our friends on the Right and sometimes on the Left keep advising us to do. Our party is a central force in Indian life. We have the responsibilities of power whereas those who are not in the Government have the freedom and even licence to advocate courses which may not necessarily be responsible.

Our people have stood and worked as one man in every crisis which the nation has faced; knowing that we shall defend our freedom, if need be with our bare fists. That has always acted as a deterrent with those who may have had other designs on us. But if we permit this will and determination of ours to be weakened and softened by internal conflict, then no amount of arms can help us. Arms used by people without conviction cannot provide any credible backing for foreign policy. While we must have arms to defend our country from any aggression, military strength must be supported by conviction in our ideals and confidence in ourselves. Both are equally potent weapons and, without them, other weapons can be dangerous to ourselves and also useless to our defence. This is the essence of our foreign policy. If we can understand and keep it, we have a certain amount of manoeuvrability. Why do Government of India not wish to make categorical statements sometimes? Because it is not in our interest to be known as rigidly confined in any given position. When we are inflexible, it helps our enemies. They can move about while we are stuck, and we become a good target.

Flexibility and manoeuvrability must however always be consistent with our national interest and honour. We cannot manoeuvre or fluctuate where basic convictions, ideals, aims and objectives are concerned. If we keep this in view, then I think India will not only keep its position in the world but be able to enhance it. This is something that our people must be made to understand. It is not enough to reach the educated, we must go to the villages and all the rural areas to explain these matters to rural people, to tell them how closely foreign policy is connected with domestic policy and how what happens in far-away countries affects developments inside our country. Only then will we be able to have that united force which can make our country great.

*   *   *

After the split in the Congress, I was running a minority Government. Had the opposition joined forces, we would have been very badly defeated. But the Opposition was very helpful. The only people who were rude to us were those who had left us. All the others, right and left, criticized us but did not allow a crisis to develop.

Then came the problem of the Princes' privy purses. On 1 September I had introduced in Parliament a Constitution Amendment Bill to discontinue the privy purses. It was a very sensitive question. The princes had been on the side of the British. Many of them had been put there by the British in place of the former rulers. Some of them were not even the actual persons entitled to the benefits. I think it was a good thing that Sardar Patel came to an agreement with them at the time of independence and that there was no bloodshed. I don't believe for a moment that they would have fought. Had they done so, they would have been pulled to pieces by the people. What we were giving them as privy purses was negligible. On earlier occasions, I had not pressed for abolition because it seemed to me that a mere 40 million rupees was not worth the fight. But we realized that it was becoming more and more of a symbol, of a remnant of old situations and conditions; and our Party held strong views. That is why it became necessary to put an end to that system. What irritated people most was not the privy purse, but the rest of it, the fact that princes didn't pay water and electricity rates. The poor man had to pay but the prince did not. They also had free medical treatment. Different States had different concessions and many of these small privileges were an irritant to the common man.

The bill was passed by the Lok Sabha to the thunderous cheers of a record-breaking attendance. But, in the Rajya Sabha a fraction of a vote less than the two-thirds majority prevented it from becoming law. I obtained a presidential order, but the princes took the issue to the Supreme Court which, on 27 November, declared the order illegal. Because I wanted to keep my pledges to the people and although our government could have continued in power for another 14 months I asked the President to dissolve Parliament and call for new elections.

* * *

So, in 1971, another campaign opened. It was quite extraordinary. Someone even said: "What was extraordinary and exhilarating was that the elections became a sort of movement — a people's movement." It is true that I like being with the people. I shed my fatigue when I am with them. I think for any head of government, it is important to be in close touch with people. I remember speaking with Jenny Lee[1] when she visited some villages and all kinds of places (we have no restrictions). She said that she saw poverty, but that everywhere children were bright-eyed. She didn't see anybody looking famished or with swollen stomachs nor were there any visible signs of malnutrition or misery.

You can get the feel of a place by being there. I don't see the people as a mass, I see them as so many individuals, even when I go to a meeting like the Vizagpatnam one, which was the biggest meeting I have ever seen (at 3.30 in the afternoon, you couldn't see the end of it in any direction; the streets were also packed with people). I look attentively enough so that I recognize persons when I see them a second time even in a large crowd and I can tell whether they have changed their clothes. Each person really feels that I am communicating with him. But in such a huge meeting you can only see those who are close.

* * *

---

1. British Labour MP, widow of Aneurin Bevan.

We knew some Muslims who lived in a nearby Uttar Pradesh town. They were not political, but I had visited their farm once. Feroze was very keen on mangoes and he used to be on the panel which selected the best mango of the year. He had promised them that he would go to their farm, but he never went. Even when my father was alive, they had invited us many times but somehow I didn't go. Then, when I was Minister of Information they reminded me of our many promises and we went to picnic in their orchard. Later on, most of them helped in the elections.

Here in Delhi the tongawalas, taxi drivers and all such people contributed money to the party. When they knew their customers were Congress people they wouldn't charge them and would say: "On the contrary, we would like to give." I think life is always a peculiar mixture, it is not just a manifesto.

CHAPTER 8

The Leader of the Country
The Third Phase

On 18 March 1971, you were elected leader of the Congress Parliamentary Party and Prime Minister for the third time in succession. The Congress crisis, the competitive radicalism which resulted, the election campaign and its results have all continued to politicise the country to a great degree and to raise hopes difficult to satisfy.

It was in this context that the public attention was attracted to the events in East Bengal. You, however, refused to concede the demands for recognition of the Bangladesh Government in-exile. You undertook a three-week official tour of Europe to appeal to Western public opinion to use their influence to restrain the Pakistani Government. You thus tried everything in your power to secure the independence of Bangladesh without a war. But on 3 December, you were addressing a private meeting in Calcutta when the third full size Indo-Pak war began. In the early hours of 4 December 1971, you made a pathetic broadcast to the nation. On 16 December 1971, Pakistan surrendered. Bangladesh was thus liberated within 14 days. It was said that you gave India what neither Nehru nor Shastri were able to give, a decisive military victory.

PRESIDENT GIRI'S ELECTION INVOLVED THE PUBLIC. BEFORE this, nobody had bothered about any Presidential election, but on this occasion even illiterates were interested in the details of the President's election — who elects him and so on. The average citizen got to know the voting strength of the different States. It seemed at first that Mr. Giri was winning and then suddenly Mr. Sanjiva Reddy's votes started going up. The results were appearing on a board.

One man was in the cycle rickshaw and the driver got so excited and worried that he almost wanted to say: "You get off here, I am not going to take you any further."

He got out of the rickshaw and started praying on the road: "Please don't let this happen; we poor people will be finished if Giri loses."

Some people came to commiserate. Another person came in tears and asked what was going to happen; I said: "Nothing, if he wins he wins."

On 1 March, the country went to the polls. The Congress won a two-thirds majority in Parliament. I was elected leader of the Congress Parliamentary Party, and on 18 March, Prime Minister for the third time in succession. The Congress crisis, the consequent competitive radicalism, the election campaign and its results have all combined to politicise the country to a great degree and to raise hopes difficult to satisfy. But the country had greater political cohesion.

*   *   *

It was in this context that public attention was attracted to events in East Bengal. At first, the only thing we knew was that the Pakistanis were fighting instead of accepting Mujib as the elected Prime Minister.[1] He was a very sentimental, warm-hearted person: more of a father figure than a legislator. Also, because he was away during the major part of the struggle, I mean, the liberation war, atrocities and so on, his angle was different from the angle of the people who took part in all this. And I don't think he fully trusted them. But they had been, very loyal to him. Whatever they did, they did in his name and for him. So he didn't give importance to these people,

---

1. Sheikh Mujibur Rehman, President of the Awami League, secured an absolute majority in elections for the Pakistan National Assembly capturing virtually every seat from East Pakistan on a Six-Point Programme of maximum provincial autonomy which verged on secession.

but to those who had been against him and against the Bangladesh liberation struggle. That was bound to create a difficult situation. Then, events grew in proportion very fast. By 25 March, refugees started to trickle into India. From the beginning, it was a mixed flow: there were both Hindus and Muslims. It was a political matter rather than a religious one. By the time the rains started, which is in the beginning of May in that part of the world, we not only received a downpour of rain from above, but also this torrent of people who did not know what to do, most of them bringing cholera or some other disease. It was a major organizational job for the Government to arrange for their stay, their food and their treatment, while trying to contain all diseases, when they were trying to get out of the camps. There was a persistent demand for action and some people felt that we should have moved our troops there.

*   *   *

This is about the time when the twenty-year Treaty of Peace, Friendship and Co-operation with the Soviet Union was signed. Some people said that the treaty marked a departure from India's traditional foreign policy. But this is not so. In those days, the Pakistanis were boasting that everybody was with them, that the whole world was on their side. So in India morale was rather low. The Soviet Union stood by us but the treaty contained nothing to change our non-alignment. In fact, there is a specific clause which says that India is a non-aligned country and will remain so. Besides, our friendship with the Soviet Union will not come in the way of our relations with any other country. But the treaty is being used by many countries as an excuse to take a hostile attitude towards India.

*   *   *

In September 1971 I visited Moscow and then in October I undertook a three-week official tour of European countries to tell people there, that if they had any influence on the Pakistanis, they should try and get them to act more reasonably. It is then that I met Mairaux again. He was a very remarkable man and delightful to talk to. We discussed so many subjects. When I met him then and even later when he came to India, he was not at all well, but for a man of his age and health, his enthusiasm and his passionate feeling for freedom, were something which one should associate with youth. And that he did not just talk about it but he wanted to be brave, and wanted to do something, however small, made a deep impression on me.

I had no doubt in my mind that the Bangladeshis would win their freedom. Not the slightest doubt. The only question was when would it happen and which side of the fence would we be on... If only for geographical reasons, we couldn't afford to be on the wrong side. Besides, if they were about to win, what was the point of greater bloodshed especially bearing in mind the atrocity stories told by refugees and by the foreign and our own press?

Intellectuals and so on, were being singled out, and after the war, a large number of them were massacred. But we kept out of it as long as we possibly could. It was not an ordinary war.

On 5 November 1971, I was in Washington when I addressed journalists at the National Press Club to explain our position.

On 3 December, I was addressing a private meeting in Calcutta when the third full scale Indo-Pak war began.

I was with a group of editors of small newspapers who had complained about the big newspapers. An aide came quietly into the room with the news that seven of our cities were being bombed.

I returned immediately to Delhi and in the early hours of 4 December 1971, I broadcast to the nation.

*   *   *

On 16 December 1971, Pakistan surrendered. Bangladesh was thus liberated within 14 days. It was a decisive military victory, there is no doubt about that. But, what I am most proud of — not for me but for the army — is that it was so neatly done. In large part, this was due to the leadership in the army and to the excellent rapport between me and the armed forces. I kept in constant touch with them.

Immediately afterwards, I took the decision to have a unilateral ceasefire on the Western front. This was not a popular decision and a lot of people and some political parties thought we should press our advantage. This decision also was made very quickly. Had I delayed it, had I not made it that night, I wouldn't have been able to do it. I wish we had kept a minute-to-minute record of that day. I was giving an interview to a Swedish T.V. team when the first news of the surrender came. The talks had gone on through various stages and we were expecting something to happen. As the interview proceeded, I was getting the information in bits and pieces. In the middle of it I had to go and meet the General who was in the next room to give me a report. I went back and answered two questions. Then I made a statement in the Parliament. I came back and answered two more questions. Later I recorded a statement for the radio. All this didn't strike me as unusual. I just felt it was something that had to be done. While giving the interview, I was making up my mind — what to do and how. I think that being able to do several things at once without any tension is one of my main assets.

If I am talking to someone, one part of my mind is with him, but if I have something else important, it doesn't mean that I have shelved it.

First I discussed the proposal with the Defence chiefs. Then, I called a Cabinet meeting. Next I gathered together the Opposition leaders and by 8.30, we had announced the ceasefire on the radio. In between, I had twice phoned Sardar Swaran Singh[1] who was in New York. Meanwhile General Yahya Khan was going around saying the fight would go on. And the Generals were listening to him even while I was talking to the Opposition in the other room.

But, all considered, I think it was a significant victory, not only a military victory but also a political and diplomatic one. Some people have not forgiven it. Our troubles in India started with our great victory in the election, and our troubles with the rest of the world started with the victory in Bangladesh. Today my guiding

---

1. Minister of External Affairs.

principles are exactly what they were before: co-existence, non-alignment, international co-operation on a basis of equality and sovereignty, full independence and freedom from domination and fear, and work with other nations for friendship and peace all over the world.

CHAPTER 9

The Emergency and After

*The proclamation of the state of the emergency in June 1975 was
described as a real "coup de force". In any case it came as a surprise.
In a message to the nation you spoke of a "deep and widespread
conspiracy", of the "forces of disintegration in full play", of
"communal passions aroused that are threatening unity", of "new
programmes" challenging law and order throughout the country.*

*India had declared states of emergency before but never before
had Members of Parliament been arrested; never before had a total
censorship been imposed upon the press.*

Why had severe action been thought necessary?

O N THE NIGHT OF JUNE 27 IN A BROADCAST TO THE
nation, I gave the reason for proclaiming the state of
emergency:

A climate of violence and hatred had been created which resulted in
the assassination of a Cabinet Minister and an attempt on the life of
the Chief Justice. The Opposition parties had chalked out a
programme of countrywide *gheraos,* agitation, disruption and incitement to industrial workers, police and defence forces in an attempt to
paralyze totally the Central Government. One of them went to the
extent of saying that armed forces should not carry out orders which
they consider wrong. This programme was to begin from the 29th of
this month. We had no doubt that such a programme would have
resulted in a grave threat to public order and damage to the economy
beyond repair. This had to be prevented. The kind of programme

envisaged by some of the Opposition group is not compatible with democracy, it is anti-national by any test and could not be allowed. Since the proclamation of emergency the whole country has gone back to normal except for partial hartal, and minor incidents in Gujarat. This sense of normalcy must be maintained. And there should be realization that even in a democracy there are limits which cannot be crossed. Violent action and senseless satyagrahas will pull down the whole edifice which has been built over the years with such labour and hope. I trust it will be possible to lift the emergency soon.

You know that I have always believed in freedom of the press and I still do, but like all freedoms it has to be exercised with responsibility and restraint. In situations of internal disturbances whether they be language or communal riots, grave mischief has been done by irresponsible writing. We had to prevent such situations, for sometimes several newspapers have deliberately distorted news and made malicious and provocative comments. The entire purpose is to bring about a situation of calmness and stability. The purpose of censorship is to restore a climate of trust. There has been delay in news from the All India Radio and newspapers. It took time to make all necessary legal and administrative arrangements.

In the meantime rumourmongers and anti-social elements had a field day and have spread stories of all kinds. I want to assure you that leaders under arrest are being extended all courtesy and consideration.

Ultimately, wild conjectures are circulating about an impending nationalization of industries and drastic new controls. We have no such plans.

Our purpose is to increase production, which will bring about greater employment and better distribution. One of the immediate needs is to supply power to agriculture and industry. This morning I had a meeting with the Secretaries to the Government of India and stressed the importance of making the administration more alert so that work is done more speedily and more efficiently.

This is the time for unity and discipline. I am fully confident that with each day, the situation will improve and that in this task our people in towns and villages will give us their full support so that the country will be strengthened.

*On 7 November, the Supreme Court declared your election in
1971 valid. On 14 November the opposition leader Jayaprakash
Narayan was released. But on 8 December the control over the
Indian press was considerably reinforced and on 23 December there
were changes in the Cabinet and a strong man took over the
Defence portfolio. At the 75th All India Congress Committee
meeting at Chandigarh strong measures were decided: prorogation
of the state of emergency, postponement of the elections and revision
of the Constitution. "The largest democracy in the world is dead"
said press commentators. At the same time, it was announced that
the Congress Party would be reorganized.*

*On 5 January the Opposition boycotted the opening session of
Parliament. In March, the Lok Sabha, elected in 1971, decided to
extend its term of office for another year.*

*On 2 July, the United States Nuclear Control Commission
decided to send uranium to India. In July also there was a
conference in New Delhi which decided to create a pool of press
agencies of non-aligned countries.*

*From 16 to 23 August you attended in Colombo the 5th Non-
aligned Summit. It was a diplomatic success for India. The main
theme of your speech was: "From independence to Self-reliance."*

*On 16 August, the Parliament approved the extension of the
Preventive Detention Act. On 18 September, the Government
lifted censorship measures imposed on foreign journalists, but the
control over the Indian journalists become stricter. On 4 October,
the trial of trade union leader George Fernandez and 20 other
persons began in Delhi and on 17 October "People's Union for
Civil Liberties and Democratic Rights" was established in New
Delhi. It was at that time, 10-17 October, that you visited
Mauritius, Tanzania and Zambia where you proclaimed India's
solidarity with South African Liberation Movements. India got the
support of key leaders of the Third World. It was also then that the
World Bank and the Reserve Bank of India pointed out the
economic and financial recovery which had taken place since the
proclamation of the state of emergency.*

It was because we took rather severe measures that we were able to put
the economy back on an even level. Our agricultural production, our

industrial production, our exports, all these rose to an unprecedented level. We were able to stop smuggling, hoarding and many other activities which are not bad for an individual interest but which affected the country's economy, more especially the poorer people and the middle class people with poorer income. This is what enabled us to earn foreign exchange, for instance, the curb on smuggling. For the first time our balance of payment was almost embarrassingly satisfactory.

It was not only the World Bank and the International Monetary Fund but also other international bodies and individual economists who came from different universities, they all were amazed at what we were able to achieve in this very short time apart from the fact that we had cleaned up the cities, removed beggars and introduced discipline. Some of the disciplines on traders were enforced. On students and so on nothing was done, but the air of discipline infected them also so that exams were on time and universities were run peacefully as in fact centres of learning should be.

In November, the Communist Party became critical of the Government. Ever since 1969 the CPI had supported you. It helped the Government in power that year when you drove the Old Guard out of the ruling Congress Party, splitting the Party in the process. It supported you again when you declared the state of emergency. As time passed, however, the CPI grew more and more worried. It was concerned about your seemingly rightist economic policies. Your concessions to private industry, abolition of compulsory bonus payments for workers and cuts on union activity. The CPI also seemed uneasy about your son whose policies seemed firmly non-ideological, pragmatic and downright anti-communist. The CPI supported your 20-point programme for social reform, but pointedly withheld support from Sanjay's five-point youth programme. But Moscow was not eager to let its special relationship with India evaporate over tiff: the 20-year Treaty of Peace, Friendship and Cooperation with India is in force since 1971.

On 25 December, for the first time since many years you strongly attacked the Communist Party of India.

I did not strongly attack the Communist Party of India. I did want to put an historic perspective. I did not speak outside but only to our own workers in a training camp. I wanted to say that although they do support our programme which they consider progressive, from time to time they have had entirely opposing views not only to me but to my father also. They should not be surprised. My desire was not to criticize them but to give a perspective of how different parties reacted, especially because people asked questions about them: how is it that they were our allies more or less and now are critical? So, I wanted to put this in perspective.

There had also been a misunderstanding. Some of our so-called leftists gave the Communist Party a particular version and they took it. In fact, the CPI had made up their minds to fight us then. Because if they had wanted genuine cooperation, we could have sat down and talked things over. They did come to meet me, I think twice, but they came in a belligerent mood and shouted at me rather than sitting and trying to discuss how we could solve the problem.

This is what I could not understand about the CPI and the 5-point programme. This programme was not invented by the Congress. It was our planning programme since independence: family planning, tree plantation, cleanliness of cities, fight against the social evils, all this has been there since the beginning. But the Youth Congress took it up because they thought that these were things in which people could take a personal interest. Land reform is a good programme but a citizen cannot do anything about it; it is for the Government to do it. Similarly for debt relief.

The 10-point programme is a Government programme. All that the Party can do is to see that it is properly implemented. But the 5-point programme is a more personal problem where each person has to say for example: I am not going to take dowry; I am going to fight the caste system; I am going to plant the tree; I am going to see that the trees are not cut down. So if you take this programme, to what item in it can anybody object? Can you say that the cities cannot be kept clean? or that the barbaric customs such as dowries and the evil of untouchability should continue?

Sanjay did make some anti-communist remarks. He did not make an attack on Communism. The way to deal with this is to sit down and explain to him that he is mistaken and so on. But they launched a full-scale attack on him so, naturally, he again spoke once or twice more. I think he made these remarks only three times in all.

Then Sanjay made another remark because there was a lot of talk about Congress and Youth Congress collecting money. They said that they didn't know where the money was going. So, Sanjay said in a public meeting: do not give money to anybody who asks for it unless he has authority from the President or Treasurer or somebody, or pay by crossed cheque and get a receipt. He made a general remark which everybody felt was very necessary because a lot of people were impersonating others and collecting money; they were unauthorized members. But some people thought it was directed against them personally and they got very annoyed.

* * *

Whenever there was a provocation and I heard about it, I used to speak but the thing is that nobody else did. If somebody was attacking me, at no time had they really supported me in that way. Whenever there has been an attack on anybody — for instance, there has been an attack on Lalit Narain Misra, in Parliament — the Party didn't support him and when I supported him they said: you are a fool, why are you supporting him, you will become unpopular. I said: Look, he is our colleague; if you believe that he has done wrong, they can sue him; but I don't believe it and there is no proof that he has. And later on it was found that he hadn't done anything wrong.

In the early days of 1977 the Lok Sabha was dissolved and on 18 January you announced that the legislative elections would be held in March (16-17-18). Why such a decision?

The reason for emergency and postponement of elections was instability and indiscipline in the country. We got over that position. So I thought it was time to have the elections.

I was by no means sure that I would win. I was sure that we would not get a big majority. I thought that we would just get through perhaps. I did not really give a thought to our winning or not. I just thought that we did not have the elections for some reason and now that the reason was no longer there, we should have the elections. It was just that. It was a purely democratic action.

Everybody gave the credit for democracy to the opposition whereas it was I who decided the elections and I accepted the defeat very gracefully and offered cooperation. It is they who were then trying to crush the Congress.

There is no use saying that we also arrested people, because we did it in a different context, when there was a threat of agitation and when the economy was on the verge of collapse whereas we had left them granaries overflowing and every kind of stability.

Apart from the economic welfare, politically we have achieved a great deal because the unity of India was never so strong and meaningful in all these years, before or since independence. Especially in the border States we have managed to bring the people into the mainstream of the national land. Now, unfortunately, that is already cracking and in every State there is trouble.

Indeed, on 20 January 1977, you decided to no longer apply some of the measures taken under the state of emergency proclaimed in June 1975 while it, however, remained in force. Many political detainees were released and censorship was lifted. But the new Constitution voted in autumn had been designed to suit your needs for it gave you expanded powers.

Mr. Morarji Desai, freed after 13 months in prison, announced the formation of a "United Front" called the "People's Party" which grouped together the Jana Sangh, the dissident faction of the Congress (Congress-O), the Indian People's Party and the Socialist Party.

On 2 February, Mr. Jagjivan Ram, Minister of Agriculture, resigned both from the Congress Party and the Government. He was a first-ranking personality in Indian political life and one of the "Powers" in the Congress Party at the time when — until the proclamation of the state of emergency in June 1975 — the "old guard" was still in control. In Parliament, Mr. Ram was also the most prominent spokesman for the "untouchables", who represent one-seventh of the population.

Mr. Ram's departure represented, in fact, a true and new split — the last being that of 1969 — within the Government party, because he announced the creation of a new party — the Congress for Democracy.

He didn't want to say anything. He just thought he would be Prime Minister. They promised him that he would be Prime Minister.

People were telling me for a long time that he was talking against me and that he would do something. I knew that he would do it but I just didn't know the time and manner in which he would do it. I didn't think that anything would be served by putting him out of the Government.

On the last day he came and said that we should remove emergency. He didn't say it as if he really expected me to do it. He just said: I think you should remove emergency. I replied that I would consider it. For the last two days I had a discussion with the Home Ministry and the Home Ministry had said that they were bothered only about two things: one, what would happen to the smugglers if they all were suddenly released and two, how could we continue to ban the RSS? Otherwise we had removed everything.

The Presidential Rule had gone; political prisoners had been released. So, I said: since you have mentioned it, I will take it up again with the Home Ministry. And, as soon as he left, within half an hour, I phoned the Home Ministry and asked to take another look over it and send a note on it.

In fact, he was not serious about it. I think it was Mr. Bahuguna who was behind his move.

On 8 February, you presented the programme of the Government party. It is possible to detect an evident desire to attract people. In particular, you said: "The Congress has never been the system of a single individual. I must be the humble servant of the people. The Congress has always been the party of the masses; it has always espoused the cause of the poor.... The attachment of the Congress to democracy is total, irrevocable and unshakeable ... the dignity and impartiality of the judiciary are guaranteed by the new Constitution." On 9 February, the pro-Soviet Communist Party criticized various aspects of government policy and called upon the voters to vote for "democratic and progressive forces." On 1 February, the President of the Republic, Mr. Fakhruddin Ali Ahmed died.

Fakhruddin Sahib's passing away was a very big blow to us. He still had years to go as President. He was a very understanding person who had grown with his various jobs in stature. He was of course a very strong personal supporter. He has been the staunchest, firmest and the first supporter during the split in 1969. And continuously since then he had been with me. He was a little worried about the family planning programme. He just felt that we should do something about it and punish those who abused it and we were trying to follow his suggestions.

*   *   *

I believe in democracy not as democracy but because I believe in the individual. Under democracy the individual gets more rights than he does under any other system. He has greater opportunity for development. Moreover, in a country of India's size and variety, one has to make allowances for small explosions in order to avoid a big one. Small areas must have the opportunity of developing more or less as they like and only under the democratic system can the people's voice be heard, can the individual develop. But, like everything worthwhile, it exacts a price, and the price is a certain responsibility on the part of the people, of the political party.

Democracy is a way of life. Decisions should be openly arrived at, people should have a right to choose and change governments peacefully, political activities should be conducted in accordance with constitutional provisions. Resorting every now and then to the so-called ultimate weapon of Satyagraha is not democracy, nor is forcing, through intimidation, coercion, duly elected legislators to resign. Democracy comprises freedom of expression and debate, but can a systematic and virulent character assassination without any factual basis be indulged in the name of democracy? A campaign of hate and calumny was unleashed against me in 1969. But most of our press did not protest at all. There was no comment when effigies of the Chief Justice were burnt by opposition parties some time ago or when they decided to accept only a part of the court's order. The tremendous and unscrupulous pressures which were brought to bear from all sides can hardly be believed. Anyone who might be thought to be on our side was subjected to intimidation. Some of the press deliberately blacked out anything that went in favour of the

Congress and gave undue prominence, even exaggerated, to anything that was against us.

There are parties like the RSS, strongly anti-Muslim and anti-Christian, which function in the twilight and have secret constituents. They try to exploit democratic freedom only to further their own sinister aims. Those whose ideology is violence and disruption cannot be democratic. For them to use the word "democracy" reminds me of the story of the teenager who killed his parents but pleaded for mercy on the grounds that he was an orphan.

This was an extraordinary situation. Should the opposition front have been allowed to carry out its plan of paralyzing the nation, there would have been a serious breakdown. The same foreign newspapers which shed tears over our firm steps would then have gloated over our weakness. After all, let us not forget the support and admiration they have for regimes which get results but do not even claim to have democracy. For them, some countries can do no wrong but India can do nothing right.

To have had to impose regulations on newspapers does not make me happy. But some journals had shed all objectivity and independence and allied themselves totally with the opposition front and done everything to spread doom and defeatism.

The press was very much against us even before. BBC and the Western press have always been against. Newspapers like *The Guardian* always sent Jewish representatives here. They were angry on account of Israel.

Basically it was because the Western Governments were against us: because of our general policy of non-alignment, because we were the only ones, whenever we saw anything was weakening, who gave the push and said: come along, don't get discouraged. We encouraged people to stand up to them. India was taking a leading part. They didn't like anybody who doesn't listen to them and who was making a success in spite of not listening to them.

When I told Nixon that after all Pakistan was also supporting the Arab countries, he said: yes, but Pakistan listens to us and you don't.

With all these restrictions, I think we are still one of the most relaxed nations in the world. We are not a police State. We have always accepted the verdict of the electorate but some opposition parties adopt double standards. If they lose, they talk of secret links, rigged elections and so on. If the percentage of our vote is low, there is tremendous publicity. For instance, our meetings in Gujarat were far bigger than those of the opposition. Yet everyone of them was disturbed by a handful of children or students. Many speakers were hurt, including Mr. Jagjivan Ram. One of our candidates was shut up in a house and barely escaped the attempt to burn him alive. None of these events got much publicity. Is this the meaning of freedom and fairness of the press?

There are groups intent only on weakening the system by any unfair means. The system cannot be blamed. Democracy implies an implicit acceptance of certain higher objectives: the government can be opposed but not the national interest. The opposition front displayed an utter lack of understanding of this distinction. Their anger against me and the Congress obscured consideration of the nation's welfare. Democratic liberty does not include licence to undermine democracy itself. Even in a democracy there are limits which cannot be crossed. Instant Satyagrahas certainly cannot be part of democratic life. When they win, they are for the system. When they lose, they decry and attack it. We, on our part, have accepted our setbacks at the polls.

The opposition has the same double standards in regard to the judiciary. In spite of the court decision in my case, they openly declared that they would not allow the Parliament to function. Any system can be improved. Reforms to correct deficiencies and abuses of the electoral system were in fact under discussion. But the opposition front was not interested in reform but in wreckage. It tried to strike a pre-emptive blow.

The Government's responsibility is not to brainwash people, nor to lead them in one direction, but to allow them to grow. It also is its responsibility to see that nothing happens which will destroy the very basis of the country, its unity, its integrity, its stability, or its strength.

The opposition parties have to see that the Government, once elected is allowed to function for its full term. But we weren't. Right from 1971 they started making trouble. The Bangladesh crisis came as somewhat of a chance to ward off troubles for a while. But they resumed immediately afterwards.

In 1972, things started brewing again and 1973 was a very difficult year. Political tensions coincided with economic difficulties: the general inflation and economic crises were increased by the fuel crisis and, even before that, the price of grain and fertilizers and other essentials that we need to import had gone much higher abroad. So that our own difficulties, which were considerable, were increased by what was happening in other countries. In this situation the opposition saw the opportunity of unseating the Government. And they adopted very undemocratic means. In their opinion undemocratic methods are wrong for the Government only.

Anti-Congress parties were not only obstructing development but also all normal functioning of the administration and economy. There were frequent calls to stop all work. Farmers were asked not to sell their produce to the Government. Non-payment of taxes was preached. Last year, in Bihar, when hoarded stocks were seized in some villages, students of the Sangharsh Samiti beat up the officials and took back the grain. Last year the railway strike, at a time when many parts of the country faced acute distress and movement of food was of paramount importance, was another example of how little the opposition cared for the true interests of the people. They tried to persuade workers not to work but to agitate. This is not the kind of climate in which any nation can prosper or even survive.

For example, during April-December 1974, there were 38 major strikes in Bihar. These included eight by miners, 17 by metal and engineering workers, three by road transport workers, five by State government employees, two by local bodies' employees, two by teachers and one miscellaneous strike. The loss of man-days in the public sector was 800,353 and in private sector 724,642.

Similarly, the loss during the railway strike and sporadic agitations in different parts of the country in 1973 and 1974 was estimated at Rs. 124 crore. The loss to the national economy was if anything ten times more than this. As if this were not enough, they even attempted to undermine the loyalty of the police and military. Would any country tolerate a call to the armed forces to revolt? Isn't it rather strange that we did not find condemnation of such incitement in most of our newspapers?

The aim of the opposition parties was obviously to paralyze the Government and indeed all national activity and thus walk to power over the body of the nation. The situation had come to such a pass that a few more steps would have led to disintegration, which would also have exposed us to foreign danger.

The Congress does have a majority in Parliament. New legislation could and can be passed with this majority. But most opposition people did not seem to be interested in legislation but were intent on using their presence in Parliament to wreck the system itself. They used obstructive tactics to delay and block many important measures. Their entire aim is to set aside, through their extra-constitutional activity, the results of democratically held elections.

Our newspapers, for instance, are very much class-oriented. When we say we want to remove poverty it is not simply because poverty is bad — it is bad, it is evil and ugly and is a very big human problem — but also because it will create trouble for the country: if poverty and richness co-exist there will be social tension. Either you kill off the poor people, or you learn to live together, and you can only learn to live together if the poor people feel there is some amount of sharing. If they feel that the rich are there making more and more while they are being crushed it will not work anywhere. A century ago it was alright, but not today. Everybody is conscious of his rights, whether he is brown-skinned, black-skinned, a woman, a youth or a poor person.

In today's world, it is absolutely essential to eradicate poverty to the greatest possible extent, in order just to keep harmony. It can't be done immediately. It can't be done totally. But it should be done as much as possible. And yet, as soon as we bend to this task, and people see we are serious, the full weight of money, economic power, the press, industry, local and foreign, combines. They don't say they are against the policy. Everybody says poverty is bad, nevertheless they want to obstruct our going ahead with programmes to eradicate it.

Some of the press — here and abroad — are highlighting baseless charges of corruption. We have always looked into such matters and shall deal with them strictly. Those who know me have seen how simply my family and I live. I have given away my ancestral home and its extensive grounds. Were these the actions of a person who was interested in making money?

What about the supporters of this campaign? It is known that a very large amount has been spent on it. Where has this come from? The links between businessmen and others and this movement is not hidden and people are well aware of them. In fact, this is why some of these politicians were rejected by the public.

There was an American journalist who was constantly writing that it was wrong for India to go in for industry, for atomic energy, etc... One day that same person came to see me for an interview and said: "The people here say you are very antiquated!"

So far as the West is concerned, it seems to us that nothing we do can be right. Because they would like us to do things which would keep us beholden to them. Because we are saying we want to be independent. Young people don't remember this, but the worst part of being under foreign rule was the constant humiliation. Going to jail or being beaten up was a very small part of our suffering. The really galling part was that you were constantly being humiliated in your own country.

CHAPTER 10

The India of My Dreams

AS FOR THE FUTURE OF INDIA, WHAT IS THE POINT IN prophetizing. We all have ideas about our children; some parents do all they can to force their children to develop in a particular way. But they cannot. Each child has his own personality and it develops with him. All you can do is to look on. Tagore said: "Your children are not your children, they are the children of your dreams."

They have something of our dreams but, nevertheless, they develop quite independently.

This also applies to one's country. No matter what one wants and what one does for it, it develops in its own way. Its development is influenced by whatever is happening and also by the trends of the ordinary people.

I should not waste time foretelling India's future. I have been brought up to feel that India is a special place. It does not mean that the people are better, more moral or more spiritual than other people; but I think that, in spite of a great deal of hypocrisy, they have aimed at certain ideals which other countries have jettisoned. These ideals also feature in other religions but people and governments pay little attention.

In India, our ideals have mattered, even though nothing may have been done about them. They were there, at the back — not of every individual's — but of the national mind, if I can put it that way. A little presence which has given something to India.

They provided the strength and the inner resources on which we have been able to call in all periods of crisis. This applies also to our poverty. I am greatly distressed about poverty, but I think that even our poorest people have a quality which prosperous people elsewhere do not often have. I would like the India of the future to keep this quality while ridding itself of poverty. I don't know whether it is possible.

Once you start getting more, do you automatically become more greedy? I don't know; but this is something we have to fight against. One reason why people are against India is that we are the only country which talks about these matters. Maybe we have not done much but at least we are thinking and talking. We are the only country not to feel that we should just copy what is done in the West. We should learn everything we can from Western countries, and there is a great deal to learn, in science, technology and other things, even culture. But, as Gandhiji said, we shouldn't be blown off our feet, we should keep our roots here.

Ultimately, I believe in one world and I hope there will come a time when people while retaining their individualities will no longer consider themselves as separate. For instance, in every part of India, even the most backward people are proud of their culture and customs and yet, it doesn't prevent them from being good Indians. They consider the whole country as their land.

I wish that the world would regard itself as one and not be divided into one, two, three, four. The attitude should be one of helping one another and cooperating.

For that purpose, the country should re-assert its cultural identity. You can only make a contribution if you are sure of yourself and recognize your weaknesses — not if you doubt your identity. This is one of our differences with a party like the Jana Sangh. They think that Hinduism is all that is right. We say that there are very many weaknesses and we try to eliminate them; but I also think that we should not throw the baby out with the bathwater. What is valuable in our culture and tradition we should preserve and try to improve if we can—although I don't think we can. A lot of customs and rituals are added on as time passes, and may be regarded as religion. But they are not, they are just temporary. Only the basis is timeless; and the basic values can apply to any time, to any crisis.

*   *   *

The Government could also help the people develop culturally, through education. Not only in formal education (schools and colleges) but also with what is called non-formal education and which has many descriptions. We should make an effort towards a constant education of all the people, whether they be factory workers, peasants or anybody else. I do not know how we can achieve that. We certainly don't wish to do any brainwashing. We don't want to say that ours is the only right method. We want people to think for themselves. But a lot of people need guidance of a sort. That does not imply forcing them in one direction but helping them to develop. As one tries to do with one's children. We are not imposing ideas on them but we try to see how they are developing and how we can help.

One has to make a distinction: are we thinking in terms of five years or are we thinking in terms of a hundred or a thousand years? This is the basic difference between India and the West. The West thinks in terms of five, ten or even twenty years. India has largely — I am not saying that this is true of today — thought of time as eternal. Problems have to be put in that perspective.

The emphasis put on economic and industrial development is a setback to some extent. Not only does it create air and water pollution, but it alienates people: in earlier times, people had a warm relationship with their crafts. That has disappeared today. A person who is turning a wheel or a lathe has no relationship with the factory. But we are bound and limited by what is happening in the rest of the world. This is where the conflict arises with some people who claim that we are not following Gandhiji's ideas completely. In today's world you cannot develop the village without industry. If we don't industrialize, how can we safeguard our freedom? We must be self-reliant as regards certain basic needs, and today steel is a basic need. Fertilizers also are a basic need. Therefore, one is dependent on industry to some extent. This is the area that non-formal education could deal with. It could make it less of a drudge, by allowing a man to develop in spite of the fact that his job is repetitious and uninteresting.

The ideal, of course, would be for India not to develop industry alone; but the resistance is tremendous because it is the most difficult path. Nobody wants to take a difficult path. Everybody prefers the easier one. This is another advantage I have since childhood: I have always preferred the more difficult path. When we went for walks, everybody kept to the road but I always climbed straight up.

*　　*　　*

Recently, the Ministers of Culture of 42 countries of Africa held a meeting where they said that they didn't want industrialization that would ignore cultural development. But many of these countries are very dependent on other countries. It is all right for a smaller country but India cannot be. We are too big for that. If ever we are in trouble, whether it is a natural calamity or a man-made calamity, nobody can help us. Even a very friendly person can help us only very marginally. Therefore, it is essential for us to be as self-reliant as possible. To some extent all countries have to be interdependent but I think that interdependence must be based on independence within each country and that can only be achieved when you are not dependent on other countries for essentials.

Besides, we are not only taking from others. We are also giving. We assist a number of countries in Asia and Africa. Then there is the brain drain. We are contributing to the affluent countries' economics with skilled people, experts, specialists and so on, and, in money terms, it amounts to quite a lot. Apart from that, our main contribution is our basic philosophy. I don't mean all these gurus who are trying to give short cuts to instant religion. If meditating helps people, all right, I have nothing against it; but I don't know whether it helps them fundamentally or whether it is simply like taking a pill of some kind. India could probably play a cultural role in the world. But are we ready for it? Are we as aware of our own culture as we should be before we attempt to export it? When I watch tribal people, folk dancers, there is such a spirit of gaiety, of spontaneity that I feel sorry that, in giving them a better life, this may be the price to pay. Recently an Oraon tribe gave a performance here. They really are among the best of our folk dancers. They had a lady with them, who must have been an official. As usual they drew me into their dance and, fortunately, even though I was three times as old as anybody else in the group, I am flexible, and could keep up with them. But then that lady thought she, too, should participate, I think mainly for the photograph but she was stiff as a rod and upset everybody's rhythm.

Needless to say, we are trying to preserve all these arts. We are conscious that we want to keep our culture as it is, and I do my little bit. A few months ago, I was going to a bird sanctuary and they asked me to open a lodge there. I replied that I would not open it if it was made of cement or concrete. This is only a small matter but it is part of a larger design: we are gradually trying to ensure that architecture uses more Indian material and more Indian designs. And giving orders is no good, you have to take a stand. Some old techniques are more expensive than the new ones.

When you look at costumes too, the old ones were very much more beautiful. But then, a girl would spend years embroidering a skirt for her marriage and ended by wearing it for most of her life. It was so beautifully and strongly made that it lasted. Today she doesn't have the time or the inclination. The same goes for many handicrafts. It seems so much easier and cheaper to buy plastic than to spend time and labour with intricate wood or ivory carving. What a pity!

I have tried hard to do whatever I could for the revival of Indian culture from the beginning. The promotion of Indian folk dancing was at my initiative. The government had refused to help us the first year. It is only because of the Duke of Edinburgh's visit that they asked us to put up a performance and offered the money for it. That was the first of what became a regular colourful feature of our Republic Week celebrations. It was my suggestion to have floats and tableaux. Initially, there was opposition from those in charge. They felt that they would detract from the precision of the parade. But this programme also became popular and my suggestion that we should now change to something new has been resisted. The Republic Day parade has been shortened to cut down its expense.

Even for conservation — whether it be of wild life or of our cultural heritage or temples — the Government is doing a great deal. The only obstacle is shortage of money. Such items are the first to be axed.

Cultural developments in the West are very different, because there is already an economic and an industrial base. They do not lack money to spend. But it becomes very difficult when it is a matter of choosing between, say education and the cultural heritage. Ultimately, it is part of education, in its widest sense. People should be alive to these things, and feel that these are necessary to life, that our old temples, statues, paintings and books are part of Indian culture. Unfortunately, people are just cutting up beautiful old books because they can sell each picture for 100 rupees or so. I had to buy a couple of books once, to prevent the man from cutting them up. Behind the Kutub there is a hill with a tiny building like a fort. I wondered if I could persuade anyone to buy that hill, so that the fort could not be demolished and the bricks used for something else. Fortunately, it is being preserved. I get so much worried when I see some of the less important monuments being neglected.

* * *

As I said once at a U. N. Conference on Human Environment, I believe that life is one and the world is one. All environmental questions are interlinked. The population explosion, poverty, ignorance and disease, the pollution of our surroundings, the stockpiling of nuclear weapons, biological and chemical agents of destruction are all parts of a vicious circle. Each is important and urgent but dealing with them one by one would be a wasted effort.

We must concern ourselves not only with the kind of world we want but also with what kind of a man should inhabit it. Surely we do not desire a society divided into those who condition and those who are conditioned. We want thinking people, capable of spontaneous self-directed activity, people who are interested and interesting, and who are imbued with compassion and concern for others.

And in this perspective, women may have a special role to play. It has often been said that the level of any society should be judged by the level of its women. It is certainly true that a country's progress can be measured by the progress of its womenfolk. But we have to think carefully about the meaning of "progress." My father had a pet quotation about women, it was written some 20 years ago not about India, but I think it is largely true of the Indian woman: "She lives in her own time, in the rhythm of her own history which does not quite keep time with the clock of the twentieth century."

We still want to keep our own rhythm but we cannot be entirely out of tune with today's rhythm. The world's rhythm is a changing one. Why can't we women influence it and give it the right beat? We can develop it if we have the opportunity. I think we can evolve a

At the Muslim Urs ceremony of Hazrat Nizamuddin

With the Mother of Pondicherry Ashram

With Mother Teresa at Calcutta

At the Hindu temple of Tirupati

With Catholic nuns

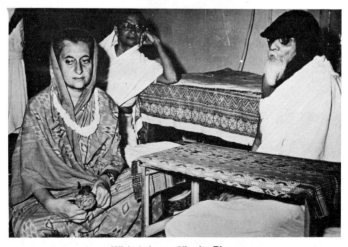

With Acharya Vinoba Bhave

With her first grandchild Rahul

At home with the family

rhythm which is timeless and always in tune. Men and unfortunately even women, are conditioned by our man-oriented society. We tend to accept the norms which men have made and even today when there is talk about equality we do not really examine it closely or consider what is good or an ideal situation. We notice only what a man does and wonder why we can't do the same. Very little thought is given to the aspect of its rightness or goodness. Men and most women are unaware of the potential ability of women. Their lives are entrapped by pre-conceived notions and attitudes from birth onwards, at every level, in school, in college and in social life. This subtracts from the total. And women are not the only ones to suffer. A lower status for women, or lesser opportunity for women, is a handicap for the growth of mankind as a whole and for men as a whole. It affects the lives of men themselves. In Tagore's great play *Chitrangada* the heroine says, speaking to her husband:

> I am Chitra. No goddess to be worshipped nor yet the object of common pity to be brushed aside like a moth with indifference. If you design to keep me by your side in the path of danger and daring, if you allow me to share the great duties of your life, then you will know my true self.

Men will not know their true selves until and unless they allow women to develop their full potential.

Women should have equality in wages and such matters. They must have better services and conditions of work and living, etc... But speaking for myself, I can say that I do not want women to imitate men, but to have better opportunities for the development of their personality.

I believe in the liberation of women in the same way as I believe in the liberation of men, that is, liberation from all kinds of obscurantism and superstition, from the narrow confines of outdated thoughts and habits. Men and women together can help to create a better society and a better world. In this, there should be no question of class, creed, sex or party.

What is remarkable about India is not the number of women who have risen to prominent positions at one time or another but that women of character have been able to break through all barriers and prejudices and, once they have done so, they have been accepted without question by the public. The Indian concept of women has been governed by two parallel currents — the visible one of the woman in a subordinate role, the *abala* or weak one; and underlying it, that of woman as symbol of energy, the active principle. Thus woman is visualized as the stabilizing factor as well as the quickening one.

Normally, when there is a discussion on women, it is limited to those relatively few of the upper strata. Women of the lower economic levels in towns or villages and from the tribal areas have, by and large, enjoyed more freedom and less social inequality. Somehow it is the middle classes which bind themselves in the narrowest and most rigid social attitudes. There are exceptions. I remember my astonishment, on a first visit to Manipur, at seeing that women not only worked in the fields and wore their textiles but also dealt with the marketing of their produce and occupied themselves with other important civic duties. What do the men do, I asked? They sit and smoke! This was a legacy from the old days when continuous petty warfare amongst neighbouring areas kept the men busy fighting and all civilian chores had perforce to be relegated to women. Women had a higher status also in the matriarchal systems of the South.

For the few women whose names are known, there are the millions of unknown who have shaped the course of nations by their own activity or by the influence they have wielded on their families. This is true all over the world, but in India we were fortunate to have a leadership which had the perception and foresight to combine the needs of the present with their vision of the future. Mahatma Gandhi and Jawaharlal Nehru consciously and deliberately drew women into the national movement, realizing the tremendous contribution women could make, in view of their numbers, and also because without their sympathetic understanding the men could not have been enthused to join a struggle which was so long drawn out and entailed such hardship and sacrifice. The number of women who went to prison or otherwise actively participated in organizational and constructive work; in picketing, processions and meetings their number was very large. There is no doubt that this, more than any thing else, awakened our people politically and sharpened their consciousness and understanding of the issues involved and the forces at work.

Our national movement vastly accelerated the emancipation of Indian women which had hitherto been the preserve of a select anglicized urban set, and prepared the ground for the prominent role women are now playing in India's development.

The story of Indian women is a varied one, for our social complex has been formed by the diverse cultural streams in our tradition commingling with different contemporary trends.

Prejudices and social inequalities still exist. Many women are unaware of their rights under our Constitution. All girls do not go to school. The average woman still has a long way to go before she can accept a position of equality with naturalness. This is not difficult to appreciate. From babyhood in the choice of colour, of toys and in manners, distinction is made between girls and boys which projects certain prejudices and preconceived notions on the child's mind, stunting its free and well-rounded development. As a girl I loved to whistle, to run and to climb trees. This was supposed to be unladylike. Perhaps, that is why to this day I am prejudiced against the world. If girls are given to understand that they are inferior to boys, and boys receive training which gives them obvious advantages over girls for employment in various sectors, it is inevitable that when women compete for jobs they will suffer from a feeling of inferiority. Many who come to public life either display a sense of insecurity or are unduly aggressive. Notions of modernity, generally imitative and west-oriented have further complicated the situation.

Many people find it difficult to understand the women's liberation movement of advanced societies and believe that in India we have no such need since some of our women have risen to the top in different spheres of activity. On the one hand, this movement is an assertion of woman as a separate entity and, on the other, it is part of the several movements and struggles of those who have been pushed around for too long.

We know that every child is formed by the genes which it inherits. Thus each individual, male or female, has masculine and feminine traits in varying degrees. Character and abilities are further influenced by experience acquired in the environment, through training and by the events which interest one's family and acquaintances. The notion of superiority of one race or of one sex is out-of-date. Hence the movement for women's liberation should not deteriorate into some kind of confrontation between men and women, nor should it lead to women being treated as a separate species. We do not wish to imitate men, we do not seek high positions for a handful of women.

What we want is true equality of opportunity to develop our latent talents and an end to discrimination on the basis of sex in training, education or in social attitudes. Obviously, there are and there will remain differences in aptitude and ability. Do these not exist between one man and another? Have these arguments not been advanced also as regards sections of men, especially Asians and Africans?

Literacy and education, however inadequate, have opened new vistas and the individual wants a greater say in family, community and national affairs. This desire conflicts with the authoritarian ideas of the older, more rigid society. Earlier, there was perhaps a good reason to have clearly defined roles for each section, and women were assigned a subordinate position. In this they acquiesced, for man was the defender and protector. But now society is far more sophisticated and fluid. There is no reason for any individual to be tied to a particular profession. All men are not soldiers or occupied in physically arduous work and many have invaded traditional feminine occupations. The increasing pace of contemporary life in the cities, and the nuclear family are compelling men to expect more from their wives, if not actually in work, at least in companionship and a deeper understanding of their problems. Education and leisure, fewer children, modern amenities which lighten domestic duties are giving women the urge and the time to look beyond the kitchen and home. Hence the time is propitious for establishing a new kind of harmony which gives the greatest opportunities for working as partners and for finding fulfilment.

Through the ages, the Indian woman has consciously or unconsciously helped to preserve, to reconcile and to carry forward our traditions and culture. Today, every home is buffeted by winds of change from all directions. How can we progress without being blown from our moorings? Our future depends greatly on whether the Indian woman has the wisdom and discrimination to distinguish between what to respect and what to reject, whether she is able to achieve a harmonious synthesis between the best of our tradition and the most desirable of the modern.

*   *   *

The India of My Dreams

What I am most proud of in my country is what I would call the Indian philosophy of life. My father adopted it as a policy but it is basically an old Indian tradition that problems should be solved through negotiation and discussion rather than confrontation. We have tried to put this into practice. Right from the Nagas.[1] It took two years of talking with the Nagas and each time there was a different representative. So we had to start from scratch again; even when we were nearing the end and just had to put the finishing touches, we were back in square one again.

But we persevered and, during these ten years, so many problems which were on the shelf were just taken down, dusted off, solved and put away. It was not all that easy to come to an agreement even with Sheikh Abdullah.

With Mr. Bhutto and Pakistan our fault had always been over-generosity. I don't know whether they understood this or whether they just thought that we were soft because of foreign pressure or something like that.

I had no special relations with Bhutto except that I tried my best to be friendly. Although he started by being rather stiff and nervous when he came to Shimla, he and his daughter both relaxed considerably during their stay. I think if he had taken a stronger line with regard to friendship with India, it would have worked. But when he started to compromise with the Military that was bound to give the edge to the Military.

---

1. Even under British rule, the Naga tribes living on the border region between India, Pakistan and Burma refused to be integrated into the Empire. After Independence, a Naga delegation, led by Mr. Phizo, asked for the right to secede but New Delhi refused. An armed movement with the aim of establishing a "Sovereign State of Nagaland" developed in 1954. It did not disband in 1963 when the State of Nagaland was created within the framework of the Federation. The authorities accused China and Pakistan of furnishing arms and encouraging the rebels. The beginning of 1975 saw an increase in insurrectional activities. In March 1975, the State was placed under the direct rule of New Delhi.

On 2 December, the Government announced that an agreement had been reached with the Nagas, ending the armed rebellion. The leaders of the underground Naga organizations agreed unconditionally to turn in their arms. The agreement was signed by six Naga representatives including Mr. Kavi Yellay, a brother of the separatist leader Mr. Phizo who has been living in Great Britain since 1960.

The same happens quite often domestically and it happened in our dealings with the opposition. When we thought that we were going out of our way in order not to have a confrontation, they thought we were showing weakness.

A French radio interviewer asked me this question: "If you had to choose one quality needed for leadership or to head a government, what would it be?"

Liking people is, I think, the most necessary quality. Only if you truly like them can you have the patience to deal with all kinds.

But, after all, what you get is what you give and everybody knows that. They say that if you see no gods, it means you have no gods within you. The conflict always is whether one wants to better just oneself or work for others as well, i.e., the welfare of the individual as against the welfare of the society. One has to have a balance between the two. Obviously if you are a better person yourself you can do better work so the two are linked.

In the field of meditation India has gone very far and very extensively. A very large number of people do some form of meditation. It may be very simple, it may be much more complex. They say that it does increase your vitality and your capability and even to do things which science today regards as unnatural; but as science grows perhaps it will find a meaning and an answer and find that there was something in all this.

In Indian philosophy we were always told that everything is one, that we are very much part of everything and everything is part of us. The contemporary nuclear physics also prove the same thing. Before we had a scientific explanation, one of our ancient philosophers has compared the relationship of the divine to the man as ocean to the wave; vibration is a part of it. Transcendental meditation is trying to do something very easily and quickly. I am told it helps to relax; whether it gives some other feelings, unless one experiences it oneself, it is difficult to say.

You see what you are capable of seeing. This is what is ultimately the aim of education — to make a person more capable of seeing and being sensitive to and responsible to the great variety of the world. Apart from this, either because I had no brothers or sisters, or as a result of the long struggle for independence or as a reaction to the tensions of that time, I have always been very close to nature. Not only to nature but to this earth. As a very small child, when people used to talk about the beauty of the moon, I would wonder: "How can they? It is dead."

The world is alive and the moon is dead. I had these arguments at the age of 5 or 6 and it used to irritate me to hear everybody speak all the time of how beautiful the full moon was. Then, of course, when man went to the moon, he just found out how dreary it was, and discovered how beautiful the earth is.

I always try to say things as I see them. This is very important in politics. This is what I meant when I said that I don't feel the strain, because I always try to be as natural as possible. I remember when I left Santiniketan, I kept up a correspondence. Actually we were a group of several girls and, usually, if I wrote to one, the letter was passed around to the others. They all lived in the same area. There were some Biharis and some Bengalis. When I went to Europe and described my travels I remember a friend replied with great irritation: "You find every place beautiful!"

So I asked: "What can I do as every place does have some beauty of its own."

As Tagore said: "If you weep for the sun, you also miss the stars."

I always try to see, and not to miss what there is.

Postface

THE INDIAN POLITICAL LANDSCAPE HAS CHANGED GREATLY since the start of the interviews in this book. At the general elections of March 1977, Mrs. Gandhi was defeated and her party, the Congress Party, lost its majority in the Lok Sabha, the control of the Government passed to a coalition ranging from leftist Socialists to the extreme right.

The defeat of Mrs. Gandhi and her party has been the subject of many analyses. It is generally attributed to the excesses committed under the state of Emergency. Those in power announced that they had sufficient evidence to indict for various abuses Mrs. Gandhi and her collaborators as well as her son, Sanjay. Various commissions were set up to determine under what conditions the state of Emergency was proclaimed, what excesses were committed while it was in force from 26 June 1975 to 17 March 1977 and how the various companies headed by Sanjay Gandhi were created.

Mrs. Gandhi and her son were arrested several times and released immediately for lack of evidence sufficient to keep them in prison. The accusations made against Mrs. Gandhi are not backed up by very convincing briefs and reflect more the intensity of the feelings of her political opponents. There is also at the bottom of all this the underhand vengeance of phallocrats ashamed of having allowed themselves to be governed by a woman for such a long time. A shift in public opinion seems to be taking place because Mrs. Gandhi's supporters are beginning to be elected to the legislative assemblies in different States.

This is why the value of these interviews remains intact. The personage it revealed will continue to dominate the Indian political scene.

It is a safe bet that Mrs. Gandhi's political eclipse will only be a temporary one.

Indeed, India is still for the most part a country struggling with problems of underdevelopment of such magnitude for which solutions won't be quickly found, at least not within the framework of a European-inspired parliamentary system. Only a strong centrist government with extensive powers and respectful of democracy while bearing in mind Indian particularity — something too often forgotten — can bring the great mass of the Indian people out of the level of want in which it now finds itself.

India freed itself from colonial domination thirty years ago. But she inherited Anglo-Saxon parliamentary democracy with carefully organized elections held regularly. The Congress Party, born out of the movement of the fight for independence had become an impregnable bastion while containing within its midst various factions each fighting to attain power. But the Members of Parliament, save for those of the extreme Left, knew that the majority of the voters they represented were illiterate, living below the subsistence level and, in most cases, their electoral success was due to one of the following factors: money, caste, religion, ignorance or, simply, violence. They represented interests which were at times contradictory but most often conservative oriented. They accommodated themselves to a system which, under the guise of respect for the rules of parliamentary democracy, was reluctant to make any radical changes.

It required several years in power for Mrs. Gandhi to break this system. Her first true victory over conservatism came in August 1969 when she broke with the "old guard" of the Congress Party. This split left her free to take several audacious steps. It was then that she was able to straighten out the internal political situation by freeing Sheikh Abdullah, a supporter of autonomy for Kashmir, to reestablish peace through negotiations in the tribal regions of Assam, to reduce the grip of the all-powerful Indian administration on the economy and increase its effectiveness, to make priority goals of technological development and scientific research, abolish feudal privileges and, finally, to undertake far-reaching economic reforms intended for the application of agrarian reform, decided on long before but never implemented, to institute a more equitable distribution of wealth and to improve the existence of the underprivileged. But this was not enough because she quickly found herself confronted by external threats. If these made her shift her attention for a time from internal matters, they provided her with additional trumps when, once the storms had calmed, to act on internal affairs without abuse of power. Perhaps, she lacked discerning advisers at this time. It is true that her entourage contained too many mediocrities with excessive ambitions, high officials or politicians, flatterers or corrupt, those who, within her own party, repudiated and betrayed her immediately after her fall from power. She was highly superior to them and her sensitivity, always on the alert, made her discover that she was alone. It is hardly astonishing that she could only find moral support and unwavering backing from her son. It was a need for this woman burdened with incredible responsibilities. Undoubtedly, it was also an almost unconscious admiration of a mother for a son changed progressively into a careerist with an insatiable appetite for wealth and power. That Sanjay Gandhi was at times intoxicated by the success and the possibilities his privileged position offered him is hardly surprising. What thirty-year old wouldn't be in such a situation. It is certain that the fawners around him made him overstep his intentions and profited from his impatience to act. That his mother failed to gauge the extent of their activities and to dread the consequences is also not astonishing since the truth was often hidden from her by her entourage.

It is also said that it was on the advice of Sanjay that she decided to stay in power and imposed the state of Emergency after the High Court of Allahabad invalidated her election in 1971. This advice undoubtedly entered into her decision although perhaps subconsciously. But it is certain that others gave her the same advice and who, today, make up all those who now repudiate her. It is equally certain that had she resigned on learning the court ruling a groundswell of popular support would have brought her back into power.

But there was in this woman experienced in political struggles the need to take up a challenge. There was also the conviction of being indispensable to her people to whom she felt linked and who had never been stinting in proving their affection for her.

The unexpected situation in which she found herself seemed to stimulate her to disregard the principles to which she was attached by an old and somewhat paralyzing atavism.

To offer the people the long-awaited economic and social improvements, called for energetic measures which could not be undertaken without a certain restraint on liberty and containing the risks of abuses. Now, abuse *per se* is indefensible, but it would be too easy to condemn totally a policy because of a few excesses. Besides, Mrs. Gandhi explained how these occurred. In fact, the parliamentary democracy system India enjoyed since its independence in 1947 had not, alas, protected the country either from authoritarian measures or from the abuses which arise from a top-heavy and corrupt bureaucracy inherited from the colonial era, or from unscrupulous politicians and shady businessmen. While the propertied classes profited from this situation and grew richer day-by-day, the great mass of the population suffered its consequences. The police in India has always had a reputation for heavyhandedness; its repressive actions are numerous and occur daily; this is the fate of a country in which the masses are poor, and illiterate and, consequently, defenceless.

In a country where demographic growth reaches dizzying proportions, the first energetic measures were directed towards a limitation of births. India was already engaged in this effort because the birth limitation programmes had, on the whole, been favourably received. In this field, as in certain others, the error of young people of the Congress in wanting to accelerate the pace did not permit the slow erosion of traditions and customs.

Finally the press (controlled by the proper-tied classes) should have been prevented from indulging in negative and systematic criticism of the energetic economic control measures adopted which were the only method to put an end to all sorts of frauds and speculations. This violation of the freedom of expression used only for the profit of the propertied classes could not have failed to arouse vigorous opposition. Strangely, the foreign newspapers, which always put quotes around "the largest democracy in the world" when speaking of India in order to indicate that a country in such a state of underdevelopment could not allow itself to be a democracy, strongly attacked Mrs. Gandhi for having resorted to authoritarian methods.

In all truth, perspective is required to offer a judgement of any value on this unusual period of Indian history which was completely dominated by a woman who has not finished fascinating the Indian people and astonishing the world.

EMMANUEL POUCHPADASS

Index